DECORATING THE LIVING ROOM

104 Projects & Ideas

The Home Decorating Institute™

Copyright © 1993 Cy DeCosse Incorporated 5900 Green Oak Drive Minnetonka, Minnesota 55343
1-800-328-3895 All rights reserved Printed in U.S.A.

Library of Congress Cataloging-in-Publication Data Decorating the living room. p. cm. — (Arts & crafts for home decorating)
Includes index. ISBN 0-86573-354-6 ISBN 0-86573-358-9 (pbk.)   1. Living rooms. 2. Interior decoration. I. Cy DeCosse
Incorporated. II. Series.   NK2117.L5D43 1993 747.7'5—dc20   92-42814

CONTENTS

Selecting a Style

Developing a Plan

Furniture Projects

Wall & Window Treatments

Room Accents

SELECTING A STYLE

Your living room, like your life-style, is uniquely personal.

The living room is often the room in which you entertain guests. Even though it will be shared with others, it is important that it reflect your own taste in decorating.

In looking at the decorating styles shown in this book — traditional, country, contemporary, and transitional — you may find that one style tends to be especially appealing. Use the ideas in these rooms to help you develop a look for your living room that expresses your personal style.

Because every room is unique, each has its own starting point for decorating ideas. For instance, the living room is often the room where you showcase special pieces, perhaps an heirloom armoire or your own handmade artwork. Pieces such as these can set a room apart, giving it a distinctive character.

Even on a limited budget, you can use ingenuity and imagination to create a room that reflects your own style, using the projects and ideas presented in this book.

TRADITIONAL STYLE

*Traditional decorating
combines rich fabrics and woods
with time-honored design.*

Traditional decorating spans many periods and can encompass furniture designs from the more elegant European pieces to those of simpler American tradition. Many of today's reproductions offer the same timeless beauty as increasingly hard-to-find antiques.

Furniture from different periods can be mixed in a traditional room; the styles and fabrics you select will determine the degree of formality. Rich silks, damasks, and tapestries are the hallmark of traditional design. Less formal fabrics include textured wools and cotton sateens.

Accessories may be elaborately trimmed. Portraits and paintings feature double matting and carved or gilded frames. Tables of rich, dark woods hold fresh floral arrangements, and the room lighting emphasizes the warmth and richness of the furnishings.

Several items shown here can be made following the instructions in this book:

*1. Refinished furniture
   (page 34).*
*2. Upholstered side chair
   (page 41).*
*3. Wall frame molding
   (page 66).*
*4. No-sew side panels
   (page 77).*

5. Table lamp (page 84).
*6. Matted and framed
   pictures (page 90).*
*7. Decorator pillows
   (page 99).*
*8. Floral bundles
   (page 117).*

MORE IDEAS
FOR A
TRADITIONAL
ROOM

Candles *(left) add a warm glow to a traditional setting. Select elaborate wall sconces or candlesticks in brass or silver.*

Picture hanger *of tapestry fabric (right) adds importance to a pair of ornate frames.*

Tablescape *(page 122) of balanced accessories (below) has a formal effect.*

Ottomans *covered with upholstery fabric and gimp trim have a traditional look. Refinish antique period furniture (page 34) to restore the original luster and beauty of the wood. Then upholster the ottoman as for a side chair (page 41), omitting any references to arm posts.*

Fresh flowers *are arranged in a silver pitcher for a touch of elegance.*

Oriental fish bowl *serves as the base for a glass-top table (page 60).*

COUNTRY STYLE

*Versatile in style,
country decorating is
cheerful, cozy, and comfortable.*

Informal and cozy in style, country decorating can have many moods. Whether the room has the look of a softly romantic English cottage or the spare furnishings of a Shaker farmhouse, the end result is a room filled with heritage and easygoing hospitality.

Handcrafted antique furniture is a key element in many country rooms. Fabrics in plaids, tweeds, and a variety of prints add casual warmth and texture. Complement the furnishings with a warm glow from table and floor lamps.

Room accents often include antique collectibles, chosen for their sentimental appeal. Quilts and accessories like old toys and tools add character to a country room. Dried flowers and informal bouquets of fresh flowers carry out the home-style atmosphere.

Several items shown here can be made following the instructions in this book:

1. Glass-top table (page 60).
2. Stencil (page 70).
3. Ivy window accent (page 81).
4. Table lamp (page 84).
5. Matted and framed pictures (page 90).
6. Decorator pillows (page 99).
7. Floral bundle (page 117).

MORE IDEAS FOR A COUNTRY ROOM

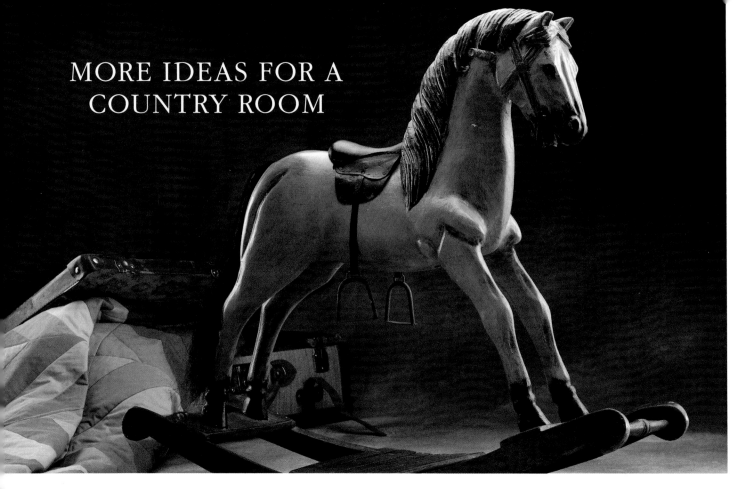

Antique wooden animals, such as the rocking horse above, add character to a country room and are a nostalgic reminder of the past.

Sprinkling can is transformed into a table lamp (page 84). Stenciling (page 70) adds to the country look.

Weather-beaten garden bench is a clever, inexpensive coffee table.

Baskets (above) in varied shapes and sizes create an interesting wall arrangement.

Quilts with a mix of patterned fabrics (right) are often displayed in country rooms. Floral and plaid upholstery fabrics add to the lively effect. The ottoman is easily upholstered, using the same techniques as for the side chairs on page 41.

Collector's tea service, arranged on a Shaker tray, suggests the charm of country hospitality.

CONTEMPORARY STYLE

Contemporary decorating,
uncomplicated in style,
produces a refined living space.

Dramatic in style, the items in a contemporary room are set off against understated background colors and low-profile window treatments, creating a sense of harmony and ease. The final effect is both sophisticated and refined.

Simplicity is key in a contemporary living room, so each element receives the attention it deserves. Low furniture arrangements are frequently used to give the room an open, uncrowded feeling. Clean-lined upholstered pieces and modular seating arrangements can soften the look.

Room accessories often include one-of-a-kind art pieces, carefully selected for their drama, color, and sculptural appeal. Indirect light, deflected from the ceiling and walls, can add to the drama of a contemporary room setting.

Several items shown here can be made following the instructions in this book:

1. *Upholstered ottomans (page 49).*
2. *Glass-top table (page 60).*
3. *Matted and framed picture (page 90).*
4. *Decorator pillow (page 99).*
5. *Handmade paper accents (page 108).*
6. *Willow arrangement (page 120).*

MORE IDEAS FOR A CONTEMPORARY ROOM

Glass-top table *(page 60) has a Lucite® cube base. The cube, set at an angle, can be filled with wooden blocks or other items of interest.*

Lamps, *in contemporary decorating, serve as accessories as well as sources of light. Flood the wall with light from a purchased sconce (top right). Or provide task lighting with a lamp made from a vase (bottom right), as on page 84.*

Handmade paper collage *(page 108) has dimensional interest. Wire mesh was used as a base for the handmade papers.*

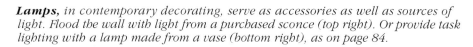

Tablescape (page 122) displays a mix of contemporary accessories.

Matting (page 90) creates an asymmetrical border for contemporary artwork, as shown at left. Simple geometric designs are painted on the mat.

Painted floor cloth (page 104) is a contemporary artwork piece.

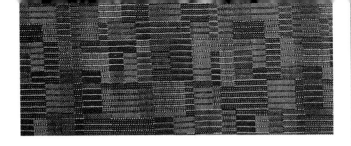

TRANSITIONAL STYLE

*Transitional decorating
combines old and new
for a fresh, interesting look.*

Personal in style, transitional decorating pulls together furnishings from several eras. Carefully mixed pieces can give a transitional room a unique flair not always found in decorating schemes limited to one style.

In a transitional living room, an understated background allows individual pieces to stand out, and uncomplicated window treatments are often used. Choose large pieces of furniture that have simple, straight lines. For contrast, add smaller pieces with soft, curved lines, such as carved-wood tables and chairs.

Room accessories may be limited to a few outstanding pieces. Items that contrast in style, such as antique plates and contemporary paintings, add emphasis and drama. To keep the lighting low-key, use recessed or unobtrusive architectural fixtures to provide general lighting, and use simple table lamps for task lighting.

Several items shown here can be made following the instructions in this book:

*1. Upholstered side chair
   (page 41).*
*2. Frame-style table
   (page 55).*
*3. Grommet panels with
   lacing (page 78).*
4. Table lamp (page 84).

*5. Matted and framed
   picture (page 90).*
*6. Decorator pillows
   (page 99).*
*7. Painted floor cloth
   (page 104).*

MORE IDEAS FOR
A TRANSITIONAL ROOM

Wrought-iron curtain rod *(above and on page 19) adds texture and interest. Businesses that specialize in ornamental metal work can shape an iron rod to your specifications.*

Collection of art *(left) from around the world gains in importance and impact when displayed as a grouping.*

Pendulum clock *(below) works well for a transitional room, because its traditional design has been updated with contemporary materials.*

Transitional lamp *(below) is made from a pottery vase, as on page 84. The vase is supported on an iron frame.*

Persian rug *adds exotic, old-world charm to a transitional room.*

Ornate brackets *support a glass shelf, on which traditional and contemporary pieces are combined for a unique, transitional effect.*

Floral bundle *(page 117) combines country-style elements with a contemporary sculptural arrangement, resulting in a transitional look.*

Developing
a Plan

PLANNING THE ROOM

Room layout *can be easier to plan with cut-to-scale furnishings. Project planning kits with precut pieces are available.*

Whether you are redecorating the entire living room, or simply sprucing up an existing decorating scheme, develop a working plan for the project. The inspiration can come from many sources. Notice what you like as you browse through books and magazines and as you visit decorating studios or homes.

Decide on the decorating style and the level of formality you want, keeping in mind the style of furnishings that makes you feel most comfortable. You may prefer an elegant traditional style or a more casual country look.

Note the architectural detailing in the room; elaborate cove moldings are traditional in styling, while oak chair railing suggests a country influence. Keep in mind that styles can be mixed for a transitional decorating scheme.

Contemporary furnishings can be a striking contrast to traditional architecture.

When planning the layout of the room, strive to make the room aesthetic and to create a functional plan that suits your family's needs. It is helpful to visualize the room empty, because the space itself will influence how you approach a decorating plan.

The way you position the furnishings in the room can play up some elements and minimize others. Plan for a balanced arrangement of furniture with one dominant focal point. The focal point may be an existing fireplace or a window with an exeptional view. Or it may be an added piece, such as a striking painting or a large or unusual piece of furniture.

IDEAS FOR ROOM LAYOUTS

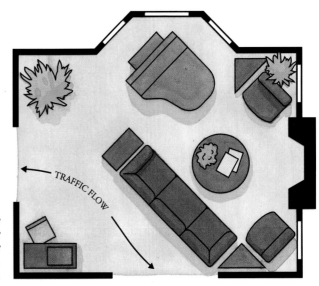

Natural traffic patterns *serve as a guide to furniture placement in a room. Notice how people move within the room and from one room to another, and position the furniture to direct the traffic flow, as shown at right, preventing disrupted conversations.*

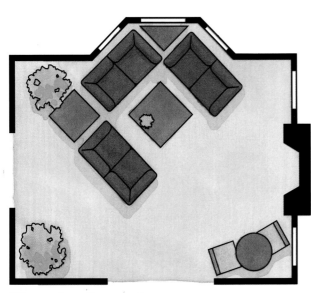

Diagonal seating group *can enliven a room and provide an inviting conversation area. For good conversation, the distance between seats should not exceed eight feet (2.48 m).*

Extra side chairs *may be placed in the corners of the room, allowing for individual seating. These chairs may be drawn into the conversation area when you entertain large groups of people.*

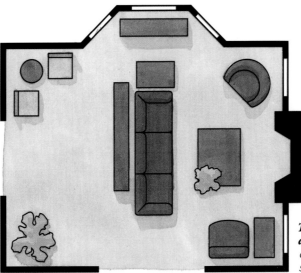

Two or more seating areas *are suggested to create a more intimate setting in a large room.*

COLORS, PATTERNS & TEXTURES

Accessories in contrasting colors add vitality to an otherwise subdued room. Above, the neutral furnishings are highlighted with bright, warm accent colors. Below, black accessories add more daring, striking contrast.

Colors influence the overall look of a room, making it warm and cozy, or refreshingly cool. Choose a color scheme based on your personal preferences, the mood you want to create, and the lighting in the room.

The starting point for selecting a color scheme can be a special painting, an Oriental rug, or the fabric you want to use for the draperies or sofa. A decorator fabric works well as the starting point, because the fabric designer has already selected a palette of colors, and other home decorating items may be available in those colors.

Choose which of the fabric colors you want to play up, and use them elsewhere in the room. To create more interest, use different amounts of each color. The most muted color or the color lightest in value is often used for the large areas of the room, such as the walls, and a brighter color is used for the floor and window treatments. Save the brightest or strongest color for accent pieces.

Repeat the same color in various items, so the room is unified, but add interest to the room by mixing textured surfaces with smooth ones. For example, one of the colors in an oil painting may be repeated in a smooth-surfaced ceramic vase and the nubby fabric of a side chair. Variations in texture are especially important if you have selected a neutral or monochromatic color scheme. The texture of dried natural bouquets or polished woods can add a lively quality to subtle colors.

When accessorizing a room, you need not select items that match exactly. In fact, it is often more interesting if the color shades vary somewhat, yet blend well together.

Textural variations make a neutral color scheme more dramatic. Shown at left, the smooth leather chair contrasts with a suede pillow. The curly willow branches in a wicker basket and the earthenware lamp add dimensional interest.

Mixed patterns can be successfully combined. Select one pattern as the primary fabric in the room, with additional stripes, florals, or plaids as secondary and accent fabrics. Vary the scale of the patterns, keeping in mind where the fabrics will be used. Small prints enliven a limited space, but can lose their impact if used for a large item, such as a sofa or draperies.

Painting inspired the color scheme for the vivid accessories in this room.

Unrelated furnishings can be unified with color. Here, the colors in the traditional wing chair and area rug were selected for the country table and the contemporary lamp.

PLANNING
THE LIGHTING

A creative and well-planned lighting scheme is an essential part of decorating. Rooms that combine several types of lighting and light levels are much more interesting than centrally lit rooms. Effective lighting schemes can enhance the furnishings, make the room more inviting, and add drama.

There are three basic categories of lighting: general, task, and accent. All three are usually included within a room. General lighting provides a low level of light throughout the room. Task lighting serves to illuminate reading or work areas. Accent lighting is used to draw attention to special items, such as artwork, or create a mood in the room.

TYPES OF LIGHT FIXTURES

Your need for general, task, or accent lighting will help you decide on the type of light fixture to choose for each area of the room. Torchières and sconces can be a leading source of general lighting, while table lamps are often used for task or accent lighting. Some types of lamps, such as swing-arm lamps and pharmacy lamps, offer flexibility by allowing you to adjust the direction of the light.

Light fixtures not only brighten the room, they can also serve as accessories. Crystal, brass, and porcelain lamps complement traditional rooms, while painted metals and chrome fixtures are often contemporary in styling. Rustic materials like wrought iron and wood are often used for country decorating.

In selecting a lamp, consider the style of the lamp shade, not only for its design, but for its function as well. A lamp shade serves to direct the light where you want it. Light-colored cloth or plastic shades filter the light, while black paper shades or metal shades block the light source, directing it upward or downward.

TYPES OF LIGHT BULBS

When selecting lamps, consider whether you want incandescent, halogen, or fluorescent light. Each type of light bulb has its own advantages.

Incandescent bulbs give off warm light. Used for all styles of decorating, the warm glow of incandescent lighting is especially effective in emphasizing the warmth and richness of traditional and country styles. Consequently most traditional and country lamps are designed for incandescent bulbs.

Halogen bulbs produce light that closely resembles natural daylight. Although small in size, they burn hotter and three times brighter than incandescent bulbs; a 20-watt halogen bulb gives off as much light as a 60-watt incandescent bulb. The initial cost of halogen bulbs is more; however, they last longer and often require only 12 volts of power. These small bulbs can allow for a controlled light beam for task lighting or to highlight artwork. In torchière lamps, higher-wattage halogen bulbs provide a wide, soft beam of light. Many contemporary lamps are designed for halogen bulbs, but this type of lighting is also used for other decorating styles.

Fluorescent bulbs are an economical lighting option, used primarily when energy conservation is a concern. Available in warm or cool, fluorescent bulbs do not give out as much heat as incandescent or halogen bulbs. A table lamp designed for incandescent lighting can be adapted for use with a compact fluorescent bulb.

Look at the room arrangement, and determine where lighting is needed. For example, task lights for reading are often needed next to sofas and chairs, while general lighting is necessary to brighten and fill any corners of the room that would otherwise be dark or in shadow. Accent lighting completes the lighting scheme by adding drama and impact.

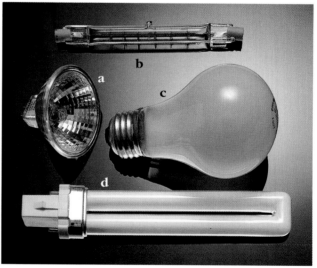

Types of light bulbs include halogen bulbs, with reflectors **(a)** or without **(b)**; incandescent bulbs **(c)**; and compact fluorescent bulbs **(d)**.

Task lighting. *Table lamps are frequently used for task lighting, with the bottom of the shade falling between your eye level and your shoulder. A tapered lamp shade throws more light downward onto the work area than upward; a good reading lamp should throw about 60 percent of its light downward.*

Accent lighting. *A small lamp can spotlight the items of a tablescape without being obtrusive.*

General lighting. *Torchière lamps offer good general lighting and are often used to brighten a dark corner of the room. They throw the light upward to the ceiling and out onto the walls.*

MORE IDEAS FOR LIGHTING

Trio of pendant lights *hangs over a side table, casting low light on the accessories in the tablescape (page 122). The unique styling of the light fixtures adds a decorative flair to the arrangement.*

Track lighting *provides general wall lighting, with individual cubes positioned to highlight special art pieces. The halogen lights in this track system are especially effective for adding sparkle to glassware accessories.*

Uplight, *hidden behind a plant, casts a dramatic pattern of light on the walls and ceiling. The small, canister-style fixture, shown at right, is easily concealed.*

Candlestick lamps with a warm glow are in keeping with the warm colors of the room above.

Sconces set the mood and create drama in the room at left, while increasing the overall light level.

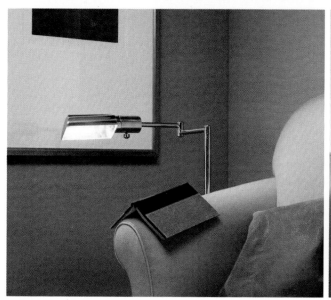 

Pharmacy lamp, *placed at the end of a sofa, provides light for reading (left). With the shade turned toward the wall, the same lamp spotlights the picture (right).*

REFINISHING FURNITURE

By refinishing old furniture, you can add these pieces to your living room inexpensively. Use garage-sale and flea-market finds or attic pieces to add personality to your decorating scheme.

When choosing furniture for refinishing, select pieces that are sturdy and well built. Look for signs of quality construction, such as drawers with dovetailed joints and mortise-and-tenon joint frame construction. Heavy pieces are generally an indication of solid wood construction. If possible, determine the type of wood. If the furniture has warped boards, cracks, or missing parts, it may require professional repair.

If an item has been painted, try to determine whether the paint was applied over the bare wood or over a coat of varnish. It is difficult to remove all the paint from the grain of a piece that was painted over bare wood, even with extensive sanding; these pieces may have to be repainted. Items that have been painted over varnish will generally have an attractive wood underneath.

There are two methods for chemically removing old finishes. Use a refinisher to dissolve varnish, lacquer, and shellac finishes without removing the original stain. Use a stripper to remove paint, varnish, lacquer, shellac, or polyurethane finishes. A refinisher is generally preferable to a stripper, because it is easier to use and it preserves the authentic quality of the piece.

If you want to change the stain color, use a stripper. Sanding may also be necessary to remove any stain that has penetrated the wood. Since it is difficult to remove all the stain from the grain, it is often necessary to restain the wood in a color that is darker than the original stain.

Strippers are available in several forms. The thicker consistencies are best for vertical surfaces. A liquid form works well for hard-to-reach corners and carvings; it also works well as the final coat of stripper, once the majority of the old finish has been removed. Water-wash strippers are noncaustic and easy to use; however, they take longer, and water rinsing may raise the grain of the wood and have a damaging effect on any water-based glues used in the frame construction.

If stripping does not satisfactorily remove the original finish or if the quality of the wood is unsatisfactory, apply an enamel paint. Oil-based enamels are more durable than latex enamels, and the glossier the finish of a paint, the more durable it is. On some furniture pieces, you may want to consider using both painted and stained finishes, painting a blemished tabletop and staining the legs, for example.

For a finish that is easy to apply over stain and that offers good protection, use tung oil. Tung oil darkens the wood and enhances the grain for an attractive, hand-rubbed finish. If a very durable finish over stain or paint is desired, apply a good-quality varnish.

When refinishing furniture, work in a well-ventilated area and avoid breathing particles or vapors; you may want to wear a painter's mask or respirator. Wear rubber gloves and protective eyewear. Protect the work surface with several layers of newspaper; do not use a plastic drop cloth.

MATERIALS

GENERAL SUPPLIES
- Solvent-resistant gloves.
- Old metal pan or wide-mouth glass jar.
- Tack cloth.
- Newspaper; soft, absorbent white rags.
- Mineral spirits, for cleanup.

FOR STRIPPING
- Stripper.
- #0 steel wool; 100-grit and 220-grit sandpaper.
- Old natural-bristle paintbrush; putty knife.

FOR REFINISHING
- Refinisher.
- #0000 steel wool.
- Paper towels.

FOR STAINING
- Wood stain.

FOR PAINTING
- Wood primer.
- Oil-based enamel or latex paint; paintbrush.
- 220-grit sandpaper.

FOR TUNG-OIL FINISH
- Tung oil.
- #0000 steel wool; 220-grit sandpaper.

FOR VARNISH FINISH
- Sanding sealer.
- Varnish.
- 220-grit sandpaper; foam brushes.

Wash furniture thoroughly before refinishing it, using soapy water and a rag; wring rag well to avoid excess water. Wash an extremely dirty or greasy piece with a small amount of trisodium phosphate detergent.

Disassemble furniture as much as possible. Remove any hardware, such as knobs and hinges, and upholstery.

Test the products you intend to use in an inconspicuous spot, such as on the bottom or back of the piece.

Prevent scratching the wood with the putty knife by rounding the corners of the knife; file the corners, using a metal file or coarse sandpaper.

Sand any curved or small areas, using a strip of sandpaper folded in thirds.

Sand the flat areas, using a sanding block. Make a sanding block by gluing felt to the bottom and sides of scrap lumber; cut sandpaper to wrap around the block.

HOW TO REGLUE & REINFORCE JOINTS

1 Regluing. Separate loose joint slightly, using hammer and a piece of scrap lumber to protect wood surface.

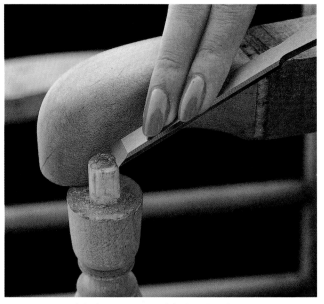

2 Remove old glue, using a chisel or knife; scratch the surfaces to expose raw wood, using a coarse file.

3 Apply wood glue to both surfaces; press together. Wipe off the excess glue. Secure joint with fabric strips, clamps, or weights.

Reinforcing. Apply metal angle plate to the back or underside of the piece where metal plate will not show; predrill screw holes.

HOW TO REFINISH FURNITURE USING A STRIPPER

1 Pour a small amount of stripper into container. Using a paintbrush and working in one direction, apply the stripper liberally to area no larger than 36" (91.5 cm).

2 Allow the stripper to soften the finish for the length of time recommended by the manufacturer; stripper works as long as it is wet and usually removes one layer at a time. Using putty knife, scrape off finish, working in direction of wood grain; if finish does not lift easily, allow stripper to work longer. Wipe the removed finish onto newspaper or piece of cardboard.

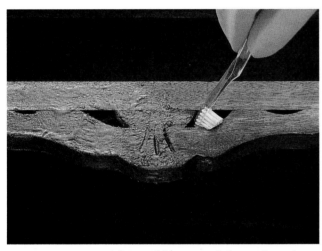

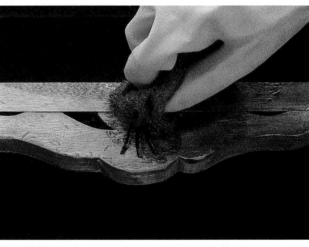

3 Repeat steps 1 and 2 until bare wood shows through. Remove finish from hard-to-reach or stubborn areas, using an old toothbrush or a soft, brass-bristle brush.

4 Rub the stripped surface with #0 steel wool to remove excess finish and stripper.

5 Apply a thin layer of stripper, using #0 steel wool, to area about 12" (30.5 cm) square, removing any remaining residue. Wipe with paper towel. Allow to dry thoroughly. If necessary, sand the wood, using 100-grit sandpaper, to remove any imperfections in wood or remaining traces of stain or paint. Repair any loose joints, opposite.

6 Sand wood, using 220-grit sandpaper, for clean, smooth surface; wipe with tack cloth.

(Continued)

HOW TO REFINISH FURNITURE USING A STRIPPER (CONTINUED)

7 Stain. Apply stain, using rag; rub stain into wood for smooth, even appearance. Allow to dry; reapply if darker color is desired. Allow stain to dry overnight. Apply tung oil or varnish, opposite.

7 Paint. Apply wood primer in the direction of the wood grain. Apply paint in direction of wood grain; lightly feather brush strokes. Allow paint to dry overnight. Lightly sand wood, using 220-grit sandpaper; wipe with tack cloth. Apply second coat. If desired, apply varnish, opposite.

HOW TO REFINISH FURNITURE USING A REFINISHER

1 Pour small amount of refinisher into container. Tear off about one-third of #0000 steel wool pad; dip into the refinisher, and squeeze out excess. Rub the pad lightly in a circular motion, working in small area; the old finish will dissolve and accumulate on pad.

2 Rinse pad in refinisher, and continue to remove finish. When the area is clean, begin new area, continuing until entire piece is completed. Refill pan with refinisher and replace pad as necessary.

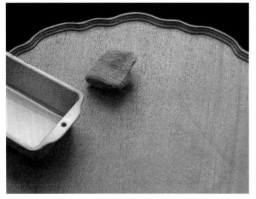

3 Remove any overlap marks and remaining finish, using clean refinisher and pad.

4 Repeat step 3 until there are no shiny areas and finish has an even appearance. On final application, wipe surface with paper towel to absorb any remaining residue. If desired, apply stain, using rag; allow to dry overnight. Apply tung oil or varnish, opposite.

HOW TO APPLY TUNG OIL

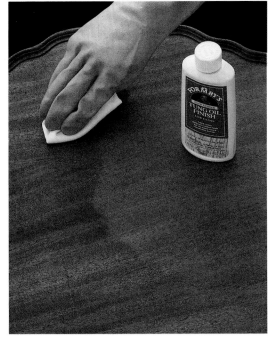

2 Buff lightly in the direction of wood grain, using #0000 steel wool; wipe with a tack cloth. Apply a second coat of tung oil. For more sheen, apply additional coats, sanding lightly between coats.

1 Apply tung oil to rag; rub a thin coat of tung oil into wood, working in small area. Allow to dry 24 hours.

3 Buff surfaces lightly, using #0000 steel wool, after final coat is dry.

HOW TO APPLY VARNISH

1 Wipe stained or painted surface with a tack cloth. Brush on an even coat of sanding sealer; allow to dry. Sand lightly, using 220-grit sandpaper.

2 Pour a small amount of varnish into a container. Using a sponge brush and working in one direction, apply varnish in the direction of wood grain. Allow to dry.

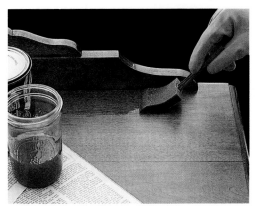

3 Sand lightly in the direction of wood grain, using 220-grit sandpaper; wipe with a tack cloth. Apply a second coat of varnish; allow to dry. If desired, sand lightly and apply third coat.

UPHOLSTERED SIDE CHAIRS

Small side chairs, often referred to as pull-up chairs, provide convenient extra seating when entertaining guests. Whether yours is an estate-sale find or an attic piece, it can be restored to like-new condition by refinishing the wood (page 34) and replacing the upholstery.

Chairs with boxed seats and inset backs, often framed with exposed decorative wood, can be upholstered, using the basic techniques on pages 42 to 47. Although the techniques can be varied somewhat with the style of the chair, these methods are used for most chair frames. A chair that originally had a pullover-style seat or loose boxed cushion can be upholstered instead with a boxed seat.

For an inset back, the fabric is stapled in place over upholstery batting. To conceal the staples and the raw edges of the fabric, a decorative trim, such as double welting (page 47) or purchased gimp, is glued in place.

The boxed seat of the chair is upholstered with a seat top and a boxing strip; single welting is inserted into the upper seam. The lower edge of the fabric may be pulled to the bottom of the frame, as shown below. Or to expose a decorative wood frame (opposite), the lower edge may be tacked to the sides of the frame and covered with a row of double welting or gimp trim.

Strip the old fabric from the chair, removing the staples or tacks with a screwdriver and a needlenose pliers, and refinish the wood, if necessary, before you begin upholstering.

Before upholstering the seat, secure webbing strips, burlap, and foam to the seat of the chair frame as for the ottoman on page 49. Use three or four webbing strips in each direction, allowing enough strips so they fit without overlapping and are not more than 1" (2.5 cm) apart. During construction, webbing strips are also applied to the back of the chair, following the same guidelines for spacing.

Side chair (above) is upholstered with a boxed seat that wraps under the chair frame. The inset chair back is trimmed with double welting.

Side chair (opposite) has a decorative frame around the inset chair back and at the lower edge of the boxed seat. Double welting trims the seat, back, and arm posts.

MATERIALS

- Decorator fabric; 2 yd. (1.85 m) is sufficient for most side chairs.
- Cording, 5/32" (3.8 mm) diameter, with single welting and optional double welting.
- Braid trim, such as gimp, if desired.
- 2 yd. (1.85 m) polyester or cotton upholstery batting, 27" (68.5 cm) wide.
- Jute upholstery webbing, 4" (10 cm) wide.
- Burlap, for reinforcing the seat and back.
- 1 yd. (0.95 m) cambric or muslin, for dust cover on bottom of chair.
- Polyurethane foam in 3" or 4" (7.5 or 10 cm) thickness, depending on style of chair; foam adhesive.
- Hot glue gun and glue sticks, or white craft glue.
- Heavy-duty stapler (electric stapler is recommended); 3/8" or 1/2" (1 or 1.3 cm) staples.

FOR SEAT OF CHAIR

Cut webbing strips 4" (10 cm) longer than the chair frame; cut a piece of burlap 3" (7.5 cm) larger than the frame. Cut cambric or muslin 2" (5 cm) larger than the bottom of the chair. Cut the fabric and the polyurethane foam for the seat top as in step 2, below.

Cut the length of the boxing strip equal to the distance around the chair frame plus 2" (5 cm) overlap; if it is necessary to seam the boxing strip, add extra for seam allowances. For a chair with an exposed decorative seat frame, cut the width of the boxing strip equal to the depth of the foam plus the distance from the top of the frame to the decorative wood plus 1½" (3.8 cm). For a chair without a decorative seat frame, cut the width of the boxing strip equal to the depth of the foam plus the depth of the frame plus 1½" (3.8 cm); the boxing strip wraps around to the bottom of the frame.

For the welting in the boxing seam, cut bias fabric strips, 1½" (3.8 cm) wide; the combined length of the strips is equal to the distance around the chair frame plus 2" (5 cm) overlap plus extra for seam allowances. For a chair with a decorative seat frame, also cut bias fabric strips, 3" (7.5 cm) wide, if double welting is to be used for the trim around the seat frame.

FOR CHAIR BACK

Cut webbing strips 4" (10 cm) longer than the frame; cut one rectangle of burlap, 5" (12.5 cm) larger than the frame opening. Cut two rectangles of fabric, 5" (12.5 cm) larger than the frame opening; these are to be used for the outside back and inside back pieces. Cut two or three layers of batting to the same size as the opening. If double welting is to be used, cut bias fabric strips, 3" (7.5 cm) wide.

FOR CHAIR ARMS

Cut one rectangle of fabric 4" (10 cm) larger than the area to be padded on the arm. Cut batting to the size of the area to be padded. If double welting is to be used, cut bias fabric strips, 3" (7.5 cm) wide.

PREPARING THE CHAIR & SEWING THE BOXED SEAT

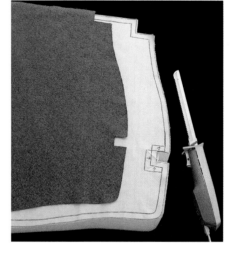

1 Make muslin pattern by placing muslin on frame, securing it with push pins. Mark muslin at edges of frame; draw around chair arms. For arms that slope out or back, redraw line ½" (1.3 cm) from original line so top of foam will fit around arm.

2 Remove muslin; add ½" (1.3 cm) seam allowances on all sides. Cut fabric for seat top, following pattern; cut foam to same size for a firm, tight fit. Apply the webbing strips to chair frame as on pages 50 and 51, steps 7 to 9; apply the burlap and foam as on page 51, step 1.

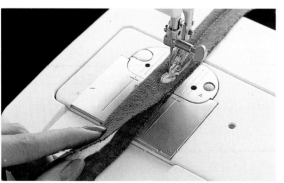

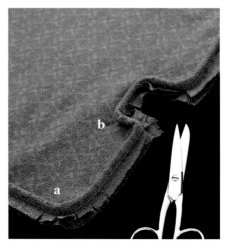

3 Make single welting by centering cording on wrong side of fabric strip. Fold strip over the cording, aligning raw edges. Using zipper foot, machine-stitch close to cording.

4 Attach welting to right side of seat top, matching raw edges. Starting 2" (5 cm) from end of welting, stitch over previous stitches. Stop stitching 1" (2.5 cm) before corners; clip seam allowances of welting at ½" (1.3 cm) intervals on rounded corner (a) or make one diagonal clip at square corner (b).

 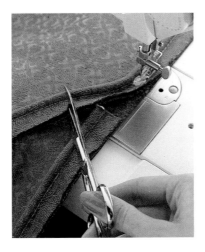 

5 Stop stitching 2" (5 cm) from the point where the cording ends will meet. Leaving the needle in the fabric, cut off one end of the welting so it overlaps the other end by 1" (2.5 cm).

6 Remove 1" (2.5 cm) of stitching from ends of welting. Trim cording ends so they just meet. Fold under ½" (1.3 cm) of the overlapping fabric; lap around the other end. Finish stitching.

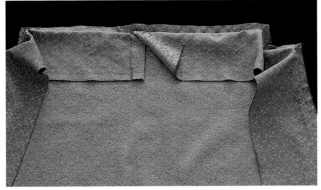 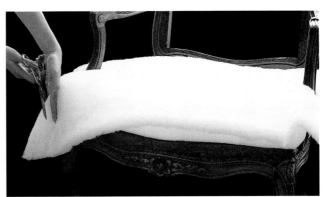

7 Fold back 1" (2.5 cm) at the end of the boxing strip; place strip on seat top, right sides together, with fold at center back. Stitch seam, crowding the cording; clip corners as in step 4. At end of seam, overlap ends of boxing strip.

8 Cover top and sides of foam with upholstery batting, cutting the batting around arm posts; trim away excess batting at corners. For chair with decorative seat frame, trim batting above decorative wood.

UPHOLSTERING THE SEAT OF A CHAIR WITH SIDE ARM POSTS

1 Chair with decorative frame. Place seat cover over batting; staple-baste boxing strip to frame at center front, just above decorative wood. Repeat at center back.

2 Smooth top of seat cover from side to side; fold back the boxing strip at arm post. Using chalk, draw a line from raw edge of boxing strip up to 2" (5 cm) from center of arm post; cut on marked line.

3 Pull fabric down around the arm post; lengthen the slash or cut a V, if necessary, for a smooth fit. Repeat for opposite arm post.

(Continued)

4 Remove staple at back of the chair frame. At back corner, fold back the boxing strip at a diagonal, as shown for chair with front arm posts, step 1, opposite. Draw line from raw edge up to 1" (2.5 cm) from center of back post; cut on marked line. Repeat at opposite back post. Pull boxing strip down at back and side of chair frame.

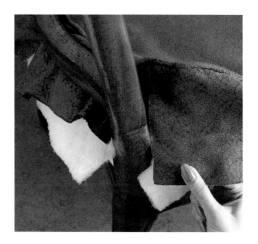

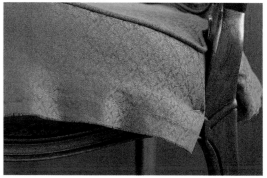

5 Fold under fabric at side of chair, with fold along back post; staple boxing strip to chair frame at fold.

6 Repeat step 5 for opposite side of chair. On back of chair, staple boxing strip to frame, working from center toward sides. At back posts, fold under and staple fabric as in step 5.

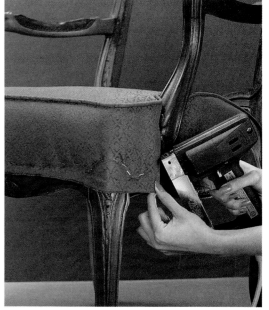

7 Pull fabric taut toward front of chair; staple boxing strip to front of frame, working from center toward sides of chair.

8 Fold fabric along the front of the arm post as in step 5; staple boxing strip in front of arm post to frame.

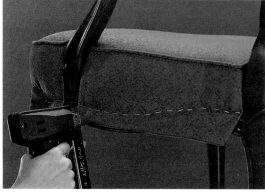

9 Fold fabric on side of chair along back of arm post; staple boxing strip to side of the frame. Repeat for opposite side of chair.

10 Trim excess fabric on all sides of chair, just above decorative wood. Glue double welting (page 47) or gimp above the decorative wood, using hot glue or craft glue, making sure that raw edges and staples are covered. Butt the raw edges of double welting; or remove cording at ends and fold under edges. For gimp, fold under ends.

11 Fold under the edges of cambric or muslin; staple to the bottom of the chair at 1" (2.5 cm) intervals.

1 Chair without decorative frame. Follow steps 1 to 7 on pages 43 and 44, except pull lower edge of boxing strip under frame, and staple to bottom of frame. Cut fabric at the front leg, from lower edge up to point where the leg and the bottom of frame meet; finish stapling boxing strip on front of chair frame up to the leg.

2 Cut fabric at side of chair, from lower edge up to point where leg and bottom of frame meet. At corner, trim excess fabric, allowing ¾" (2 cm) to fold under. Fold under fabric at front leg. Complete boxed seat as in steps 8 and 9, stapling lower edge to bottom of frame. Apply cambric as in step 11.

UPHOLSTERING THE SEAT OF A CHAIR WITH FRONT ARM POSTS

1 Chair with decorative frame. Follow step 1 on page 43. Smooth the top of the seat cover from side to side; align welting seams around the front arm posts. Fold back the boxing strip diagonally at the arm post. Draw a line, using chalk, from raw edge up to 2" (5 cm) from center of arm post; cut on marked line.

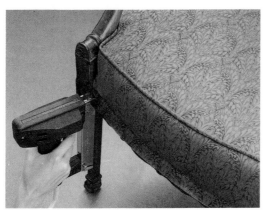

2 Pull the fabric down around the arm post. Repeat for opposite arm post. Follow steps 4 to 7, opposite. On front of chair, fold and staple the fabric at the arm post as in step 5, opposite. Complete seat as in steps 9 to 11, opposite.

Chair without decorative frame. Follow steps 1 and 2, left, except pull lower edge of boxing strip around to bottom of chair frame, and staple to bottom of frame.

UPHOLSTERING THE CHAIR BACK

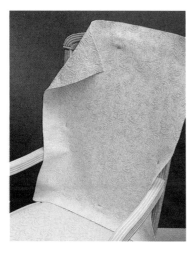

1 Tacking rail on inside back. Apply fabric rectangle for outside back, with right side toward back of chair, staple-basting fabric at the center top to tacking rail on inside back of frame, ¼" (6 mm) from molding. Repeat at center bottom and center of each side.

2 Staple the fabric from the center bottom, up to the beginning of curve at rounded corners or up to 3" (7.5 cm) from square corners. Staple fabric at top, stretching fabric taut; repeat at each side. Staple fabric at the corners. Trim excess fabric next to staples. Place one layer of batting over fabric.

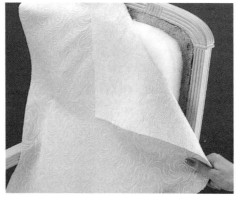

3 Apply webbing strips as on pages 50 and 51, steps 7 to 9, stapling into tacking rail; jute webbing strips do not have to be folded over. Staple burlap over the webbing; trim excess.

4 Place two layers of batting over the burlap. Place fabric rectangle for inside back, right side up, over batting; staple. Trim the excess fabric, and apply double welting or gimp as on page 44, step 10; butt ends of double welting, or fold under ends of gimp.

Tacking rails on inside and outside back. Follow steps 3 and 4, left. From back of chair, apply fabric rectangle for outside back, right side out, stapling into tacking rail on outside back of frame. Trim excess fabric, and apply double welting or gimp as on page 44, step 10.

UPHOLSTERING THE CHAIR ARMS

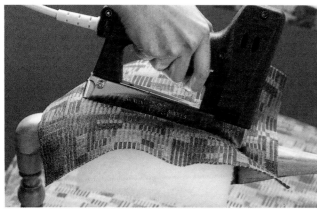

1 Wrapped arm pad. Place two to three layers of batting on top of arm. Place fabric right side up over the batting; staple at back of arm.

2 Stretch to front of arm; staple. Pull fabric around arm; staple to bottom of arm. On opposite side, pull fabric around arm, folding under edge; staple.

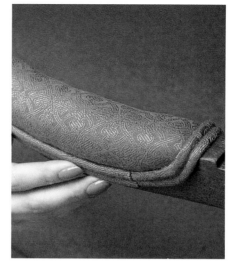

3 Finish stapling along back and front of arm. Trim excess fabric. Glue double welting or gimp as on page 44, step 10.

Oval arm pad. Place two or three layers of batting on top of arm. Place fabric right side up over the batting. Secure fabric as for chair back, steps 1 and 2, opposite. Trim excess fabric, and apply double welting or gimp as on page 44, step 10; butt ends of double welting, or fold under ends of gimp.

MAKING DOUBLE WELTING

1 Place 5⁄32" (3.8 mm) cording on wrong side of 3" (7.5 cm) fabric strip. Fold fabric over cording, with 1⁄2" (1.3 cm) seam allowance extending. Stitch next to cording, using zipper foot.

2 Place second cording next to first welt. Wrap the fabric around the second cording.

3 Stitch between two cords on previous stitching line. Use general-purpose foot, riding on top of welting.

4 Trim off excess fabric next to stitching; raw edge is on the back of finished double welting.

UPHOLSTERED OTTOMANS

Ottomans provide extra seating and can also serve as decorative accents. This fabric-wrapped ottoman is easy to make and is suitable for any decorating style. The finished ottoman measures about 19" (48.5 cm) high with an 18" (46 cm) square seat.

The frame is built from ¾" (2 cm) plywood, and has upholstery webbing woven and stretched over the top of the frame. One ottoman can be built from a half-sheet of plywood, or a pair from a full sheet. To ensure sufficient strength, use AC or BB grade plywood.

For accurate piecing, the plywood pieces should be cut with a circular saw to the dimensions given in the cutting directions. If you do not have access to a circular saw, some lumber yards will cut the plywood to your specifications.

Simple upholstery methods are used to cover the ottoman. After the frame is padded with polyurethane foam and upholstery batting, the entire ottoman is covered with two pieces of fabric.

For best results, textured fabrics with some stretch or give are recommended, because they are easier to work with. Avoid using shiny or tightly woven fabrics, like chintz, or fabrics that require precise matching, such as plaids, stripes, and large prints.

MATERIALS

FOR THE FRAME

- ¾" (2 cm) plywood in AC or BB grade.
- #8 × 1¼" (3.2 cm) and #8 × 1⅝" (4 cm) coarse-thread drywall screws.
- Wood glue.
- 3½ yd. (3.2 m) upholstery webbing.
- Circular saw; jigsaw.
- Drill; ³⁄₃₂" (2.38 mm) drill bit.
- Phillips screwdriver; pliers.
- Heavy-duty stapler (electric stapler is recommended) and ½" (1.3 cm) staples.

FOR THE UPHOLSTERY

- 1¾ yd. (1.6 m) decorator fabric.
- 60" (152.5 cm) polyester upholstery batting, 27" (68.5 cm) wide.
- ⅝ yd. (0.6 m) burlap.
- 18" (46 cm) square of polyurethane foam, 2" (5 cm) thick; foam adhesive.
- Cardboard stripping.
- Nylon hand-sewing upholstery thread; 4" (10 cm) curved needle.
- Four ¾" (2 cm) nylon glides.

CUTTING DIRECTIONS

FOR THE FRAME

From plywood, cut two 15½" × 17" (39.3 × 43 cm) pieces; these will be the sides of the ottoman frame. Cut four 15½" (39.3 cm) squares; in steps 1 to 3 on page 50, these pieces will be cut into a U shape, using a jigsaw, and screwed together in pairs for the front and back of the frame. Cut two 2" × 17" (5 × 43 cm) pieces; these will be the runners on the bottom of the frame. Cut six 19" (48.5 cm) strips of upholstery webbing.

FOR THE UPHOLSTERY

Cut one 20" (51 cm) square of burlap, to be used on the top of the ottoman over the webbing. Cut a rectangle of decorator fabric for the outside of the ottoman, 32" × 63" (81.5 × 160 cm); mark the center of each side by cutting a notch at the edges. Cut the remaining fabric for the inside of the ottoman, 20" × 47" (51 × 120 cm); notch the center of one long side.

BUILDING AN OTTOMAN FRAME

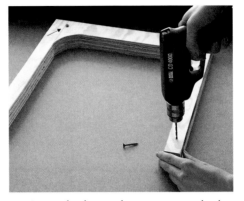

1 Mark a line 2" (5 cm) from the upper edge of 15½" (39.3 cm) plywood square; mark a line 1¼" (3.2 cm) from each adjacent side. Mark rounded corners where lines intersect, as shown. Repeat for remaining 15½" (39.3 cm) squares.

2 Cut each plywood square on marked lines, using a jigsaw. Stack two pieces; at one corner, predrill hole about 1¼" (3.2 cm) deep, using ³⁄₃₂" (2.38 mm) drill bit. Partially insert 1¼" (3.2 cm) drywall screw to hold corners flush (arrow). Predrill hole at diagonal corner.

3 Remove screw; glue the pieces together, using wood glue. Insert screws at corners. Insert additional screws at center and corners of each side. Secure the two remaining U-shaped pieces together. The glued pieces will be the front and back of the frame.

4 Stand front piece upside down. Position one side piece over side of front piece, with edges even. Predrill screw holes about 1⅝" (4 cm) deep, staggering the holes so screws will be located in both plywood layers of front and will not intersect previously inserted screws. Secure the joint with wood glue; insert 1⅝" (4 cm) screws.

5 Repeat step 4 to attach back piece. Attach remaining side piece in same manner.

6 Position runner on bottom of frame, with the edges even; predrill screw holes about 1⅝" (4 cm) deep, so screws will not intersect previously inserted screws at the corners. Secure the joint with wood glue; insert 1⅝" (4 cm) screws. Repeat for the opposite runner.

7 Secure one strip of webbing to upper edge of frame, centered on one side; fold up ½" (1.3 cm) at end of webbing, and staple through both layers, using five staples. On opposite side of frame, staple webbing to frame through single layer, pulling webbing tight with pliers.

8 Fold up end of webbing strip; staple again through both layers. Trim end of webbing to ½" (1.3 cm).

9 Repeat for two more strips, evenly spacing them on either side of center strip. Secure three strips of webbing to frame in opposite direction, weaving them over and under the previous strips. Staple all strips as in steps 7 and 8, stretching them tight with pliers.

UPHOLSTERING AN OTTOMAN

1 Fold under edges of burlap piece; staple it to top of frame, over the webbing, at 1½" (3.8 cm) intervals, stretching burlap taut. Apply spray adhesive to one side of foam and to burlap; adhere foam to burlap.

2 Mark center of top rails on lower edge (**a**). Mark center of each side at bottom of frame (**b**).

3 Place upholstery batting on table, with the frame upside down over it. Wrap batting around top and sides of frame; stretching batting slightly, staple it to center of each side, near bottom of frame.

4 Wrap batting over top rail on front of frame; apply staple to center near the bottom of rail. Repeat, wrapping batting over the top rail on back of frame, stretching it slightly.

5 Apply staples to sides at bottom, 1½" (3.8 cm) apart, stretching the batting taut. Trim excess batting at the bottom of the frame; batting should not wrap around lower edge of frame.

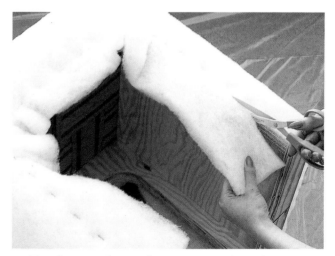

6 Turn frame so front is facing up. Stretching the batting slightly over front, apply staples, 1½" (3.8 cm) apart, on top rail and sides of U-shaped front edge; at corners, ease in excess batting and staple in place. Trim excess batting next to edges of frame front.

(Continued)

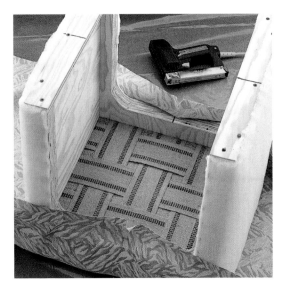

7 Repeat step 6 on page 51 with back of frame facing up. Place fabric for outside of ottoman on table, with ottoman upside down over it. Staple-baste center of fabric on one side to bottom of front rail at center marking. Stretch fabric taut, and staple opposite side of fabric to marking on back rail.

8 Stretch fabric around frame to bottom of one side; staple-baste to bottom of runner, matching centers. Stretch fabric taut to other side; staple-baste to bottom of other runner.

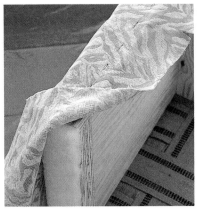

9 Remove staple on bottom of one runner, and stretch fabric tighter. Apply staples 1½" (3.8 cm) apart on bottom of runner, working from center to within 2" (5 cm) of ends.

10 Repeat step 9 for opposite side of ottoman. Remove staple from front rail of ottoman. Stretching fabric tight, apply staples 1½" (3.8 cm) apart, working from center to within 1" (2.5 cm) of beginning of curved corners.

11 Stretch fabric taut at one curved front corner, 1" (2.5 cm) beyond curve in frame; staple. Apply staples 1½" (3.8 cm) apart to within 2" (5 cm) of the bottom of the ottoman. Repeat for the opposite side of front and for both sides of back.

12 Fold three pleats in place at each curved corner; staple on the lower edge of the rail. All three pleats should fit within the curved area. Trim excess fabric ½" (1.3 cm) from staples.

13 Fold the fabric around front corner on one runner; staple in place, and trim the excess fabric. Repeat for back corner. Then fold front and back corners on the remaining runner.

14 Staple edge of fabric for the inside of the ottoman to bottom of front rail, with fabric right side down and matching centers; work from center of top rail to bottom of sides.

15 Place cardboard stripping over fabric, with edge of cardboard just inside the outer edge of frame; apply staples 1½" (3.8 cm) apart.

16 Turn the fabric right side up over inside of frame. Stretch the fabric taut toward the back rail; staple-baste to the bottom of back rail at center, folding under edge. Stretching the fabric taut and folding under the edge, staple-baste 4" (10 cm) apart along bottom of top rail and the sides of U-shaped back edge.

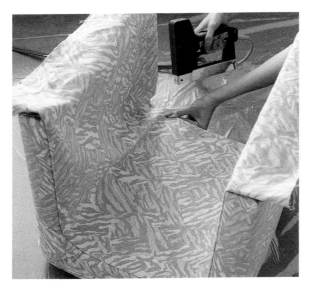

17 Staple-baste into the bottom of each runner at the center and ends, pulling the slack out of the fabric.

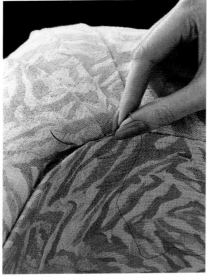

18 Trim excess fabric at bottom of each runner; fold under the edge, and staple in place.

19 Blindstitch along folded edge on back of frame, using curved needle. Remove staples.

20 Tap nylon glides into bottom of the runners, 2" (5 cm) from each end.

FRAME-STYLE TABLES

For a versatile table that is easy to construct, build a frame-style table. For the tabletop, a plywood base is framed with wood strips to form a raised edge. The framed tabletop may be used as a display area for memorabilia and covered with glass. Or tiles may be laid over the plywood, with the top of the tiles flush with the framed edge.

The table legs are cut from stock 3 × 3 lumber. Most building supply or home improvement stores have an adequate selection of paint-grade hardwoods for the legs and frame. For the most varied selection, including hardwoods suitable for staining, purchase the lumber at a hardwood lumber yard or woodworker's supply store.

For a memorabilia table, determine the desired size and depth of the display area; the depth may be up to 2½"

(6.5 cm). Cut the table legs to the desired finished height of the table, minus the depth of the display area, minus the ¾" (2 cm) plywood thickness. For example, for a 20" (51 cm) table height with a 2" (5 cm) display area depth, cut the table legs 17¼" (43.7 cm). Also determine the dimension of the plywood base; this will be the size of the display area. The plywood base may be covered with wallpaper or a synthetic suede. If synthetic suede is used, mount the suede on a sheet of heavy illustration board, ⅛" (3 mm) thick; then secure it to the plywood.

For a tiled table, the display depth should be equal to the thickness of the tile. Determine the tile arrangement, allowing about ⅛" to ¼" (3 to 6 mm) around the edges of the tiles; this will be the dimension of the plywood base. Cut the table legs as for the memorabilia table.

MATERIALS

FOR BOTH TABLE STYLES

- 3 × 3 lumber in desired hardwood, length to cut four legs.
- ¾" × 3½" (2 × 9 cm) lumber in desired hardwood, length to cut mitered frame.
- Plywood for tabletop; for memorabilia table, use finish plywood, or for tiled table, use exterior grade.
- Paint, or wood stain and putty to match stain; tung oil or varnish, optional.
- Wood glue; 6d finish nails; nail set; drill; ³⁄₃₂" (2.38 mm) drill bit; 2½" (6.5 cm) drywall screws; miter box and back saw, or power miter box.

FOR MEMORABILIA TABLE

- For wallpaper background: wallpaper; wallpaper paste; primer; wood filler.

- For suede background: synthetic suede; illustration board, ⅛" (3 mm) thick; utility knife; straightedge; spray-mount adhesive; double-stick carpet tape.
- Self-adhesive hook and loop tape, optional.
- ⅜" (1 cm) plate glass with beveled edge or factory-polished edge; size of glass is equal to the finished frame dimension minus ¼" (6 mm).

FOR TILED TABLE

- Ceramic tiles.
- Ceramic adhesive or multipurpose household adhesive, such as Liquid Nails®.
- Tile spacers, if necessary.
- Tile grout; grout sealer, optional.

Frame-style tables may be tiled, as shown opposite. Or they may serve as a display case, like the memorabilia table at right.

HOW TO BUILD A MEMORABILIA FRAME-STYLE TABLE

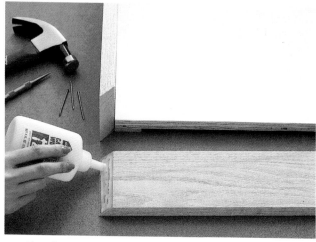

1 Cut plywood to desired finished size of display area. If tabletop will be wallpapered, apply primer to top of board. Cut frame pieces with mitered corners so frame will fit around plywood tabletop; inside measurement will equal length of plywood edge.

2 Glue frame pieces to sides of plywood, with the frame raised desired distance above top of plywood; this will be the depth of the display area. Secure frame to plywood with nails, positioning nails at corners and at intervals of about 8" (20.5 cm). Countersink nails, using a nail set.

4 Mark a 2½" (6.5 cm) square in each corner on top of plywood. Position each leg under plywood, holding the leg against frame at corner. Within the marked square, predrill holes for screws, using ³⁄₃₂" (2.38 mm) drill bit. Countersink two screws through plywood and into each leg, as shown.

5 Wallpaper background. Apply wood filler at recessed screws; sand it smooth. Apply wallpaper, using wallpaper paste; trim the wallpaper even with the edges of the frame.

3 Cut 3 × 3 into four legs of desired height. Sand legs and frame. Paint or stain legs and frame as desired; fill nail holes with putty to match stain. Apply tung oil or varnish, if desired (page 39).

5 Suede background. Cut illustration board to size of the plywood base, using utility knife and straightedge; score along straightedge until the board is cut through. Cut the suede slightly larger than the board; secure to top of board, using spray adhesive. Turn board over and cut suede even with edges. Secure the board to the plywood, using double-stick tape.

6 Arrange displayed articles; if desired, secure the items, using self-adhesive hook and loop tape. Position the glass on the table.

HOW TO BUILD A TILED FRAME-STYLE TABLE

1 Follow steps 1 to 4, opposite; in step 1, cut plywood to desired finished size of tile area and in step 2, position frame so it is raised above top of plywood an amount equal to thickness of tile and glue.

2 Wipe plywood free from dust; mask off inside edge of frame, using masking tape. Arrange tiles as desired. Secure each tile, applying two S-shaped beads of adhesive to back. For even spacing, some tiles require spacers. Allow 1 to 2 hours to set.

3 Apply grout, pushing it uniformly and smoothly into joints, using moistened finger. Gently wipe off excess grout, using dampened sponge. Remove tape.

4 Allow grout to dry about 1 hour, or until firm; polish tile with clean, dry cloth. Let grout cure according to manufacturer's instructions; if desired, apply grout sealer.

MORE IDEAS FOR FRAME-STYLE TABLES

Sand and seashells *are displayed in a small side table.*

Decorative chest *is housed in an oak table.*

Handmade paper *(page 108) is displayed over a wallpaper background.*

Pair of tiled tables *is arranged so the design of the tiles continues from one table to the other.*

CREATIVE GLASS-TOP TABLES

With a little imagination and a sheet of heavy glass, many objects can be transformed into attractive tables. For the bases of tables, choose objects that are stable, level, and the desired height. Coffee tables generally range from 16" to 18" (40.5 to 46 cm) in height. End tables generally range from 19" to 21" (48.5 to 53.5 cm).

Items like steamer trunks, antique piano benches, and blanket chests work well for traditional styles. For a country or transitional decorating scheme, try wooden boxes, sawhorses, benches, and inverted baskets or pots. For contemporary decorating, use items such as Lucite™ cubes and large porcelain vases.

Glass tabletops with rounded and polished edges are available in several sizes from many retailers of casual furniture. You may also have glass custom-cut by glass retailers. For small tables, a thickness of ¼" (6 mm) is sufficient, but for greater strength and a more dramatic look, use glass ⅜" (1 cm) or thicker. When choosing glass dimensions, you may want to check the size by using a cardboard template on the table base to determine the overhang.

Because of the weight of the glass, it is seldom necessary to anchor it permanently to the table base. Cushion the glass by placing acrylic discs, available at hardware stores, between the base and the glass. Four discs, placed at the corners, are usually sufficient. If the discs slide on the surface of the base, causing the glass to shift, secure them to the base with a small amount of clear silicone adhesive.

Ceramic flower pots (top) are stacked to support this rectangular coffee table. For a larger, square table, place pots in all four corners.

Acrylic cube (bottom left) with marbles serves as a base for this side table. A smaller cube is inserted upside down to reduce the number of marbles needed.

I-beams (bottom right), painted with aerosal paint, create a contemporary table base.

MORE IDEAS FOR GLASS-TOP TABLES

Decorative garden pot, *filled with baby's breath, serves as the base for this table. The smooth glass top highlights the rustic texture of the base.*

Folding luggage rack topped with glass becomes a simple side table.

Greek column and a stack of books balance the glass top of this coffee table.

Radiator covered with a glass top is an attractive and practical way to create a table.

Concrete bench provides a solid foundation for a coffee table and adds architectural interest.

Wall & Window Treatments

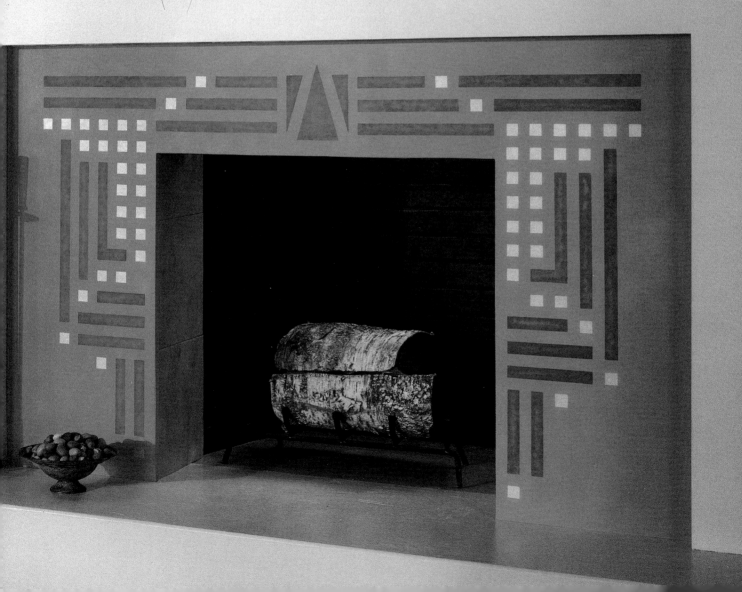

WALL FRAME
MOLDINGS

Add architectural detail to a living room by installing molding in a picture-type frame on the walls. Frame molding can be used to accent special features of the room, divide large walls into smaller sections, and add interest to otherwise plain walls. The molding may be the same color as the walls or a contrasting color. The effect can be intensified by painting the wall area within the frame molding a different color or by wallpapering it.

Crown moldings and chair rail moldings, available in a variety of styles, work well. To determine the size and location of the frames, cut strips of paper the width of the molding and experiment with different frame sizes, taping the strips to the wall. Frame molding often repeats the size of architectural details in a room, such as the width of the windows or fireplace.

Install the molding with small finish nails near the outside corners of the molding and at wall stud locations; use nails long enough to go through the wall surface and into the studs. If wall studs are not located, apply small dots of wood glue to the back of the molding to prevent the frame from pulling away from the wall.

MATERIALS

- Wood molding.
- Miter box and back saw, or power miter saw.
- Finish nails; nail set.

- Drill; 1/16" (1.5 mm) drill bit.
- Wood glue, if necessary.
- Paint, or wood stain and putty to match stain.

HOW TO INSTALL WALL FRAME MOLDING

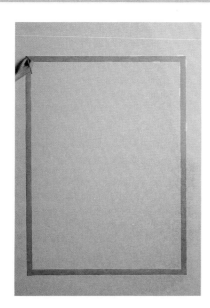

1 Cut paper strips to width of the molding; secure to wall, using tape. Lightly mark the placement for outer edge of the upper molding with a pencil, making sure markings are level.

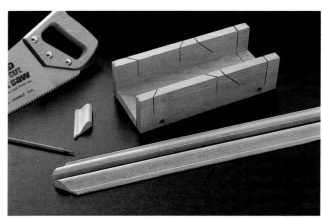

2 Measure and mark length of upper and lower molding strips on outer edge; cut molding strips, using a miter box and back saw and angling cuts in from the mark. Check to see that the molding strips are exactly the same length. Repeat to cut side strips.

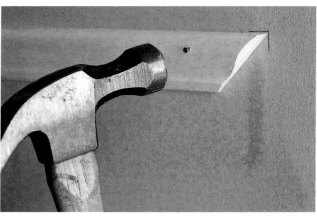

3 Paint or stain the moldings. Predrill nail holes with 1/16" (1.5 mm) drill bit. Position upper molding strip on wall, aligning it with markings; if molding will not be nailed to studs, place dots of glue sparingly on back of molding. Nail the moldings to the wall, leaving nails slightly raised.

4 Attach molding strips for sides of the frame, placing a nail at upper corners only. Attach lower strip, making sure frame is square. Secure remaining nails for sides of frame.

5 Countersink nails, using nail set. Touch up nail holes and mitered corners with paint, or fill them with putty to match stain.

MORE IDEAS FOR WALL FRAME MOLDINGS

Framed area (left) is wallpapered, dividing an otherwise plain wall.

Double molding (opposite) is used to further emphasize the architectural detailing.

Contrasting molding (below) calls special attention to the artwork in this traditional grouping.

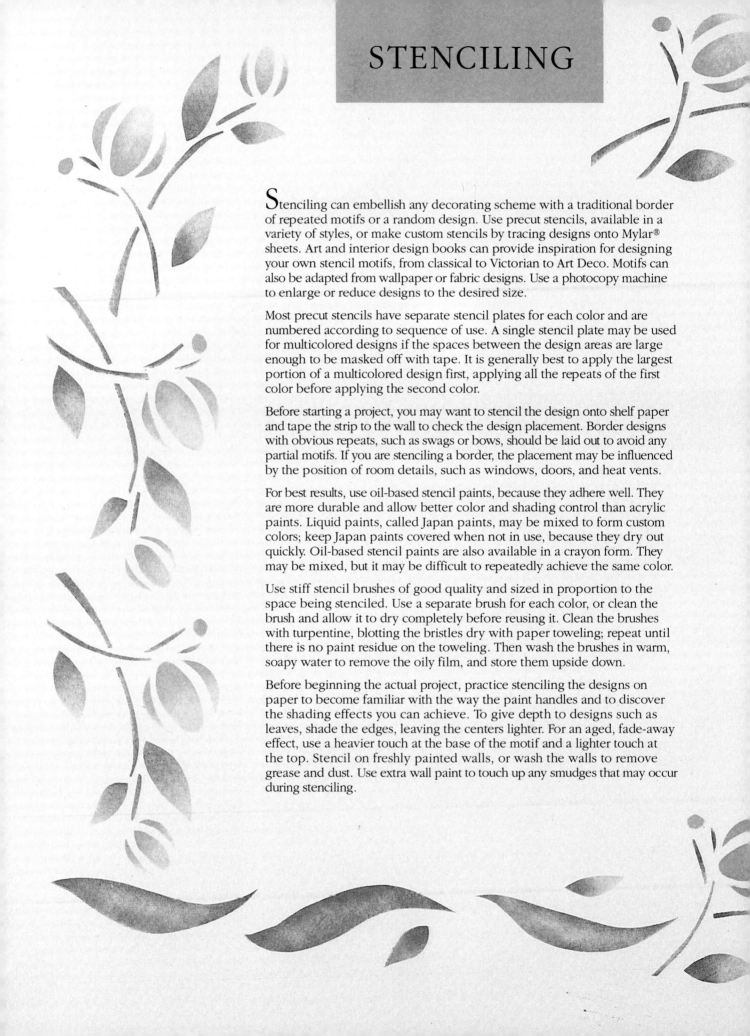

STENCILING

Stenciling can embellish any decorating scheme with a traditional border of repeated motifs or a random design. Use precut stencils, available in a variety of styles, or make custom stencils by tracing designs onto Mylar® sheets. Art and interior design books can provide inspiration for designing your own stencil motifs, from classical to Victorian to Art Deco. Motifs can also be adapted from wallpaper or fabric designs. Use a photocopy machine to enlarge or reduce designs to the desired size.

Most precut stencils have separate stencil plates for each color and are numbered according to sequence of use. A single stencil plate may be used for multicolored designs if the spaces between the design areas are large enough to be masked off with tape. It is generally best to apply the largest portion of a multicolored design first, applying all the repeats of the first color before applying the second color.

Before starting a project, you may want to stencil the design onto shelf paper and tape the strip to the wall to check the design placement. Border designs with obvious repeats, such as swags or bows, should be laid out to avoid any partial motifs. If you are stenciling a border, the placement may be influenced by the position of room details, such as windows, doors, and heat vents.

For best results, use oil-based stencil paints, because they adhere well. They are more durable and allow better color and shading control than acrylic paints. Liquid paints, called Japan paints, may be mixed to form custom colors; keep Japan paints covered when not in use, because they dry out quickly. Oil-based stencil paints are also available in a crayon form. They may be mixed, but it may be difficult to repeatedly achieve the same color.

Use stiff stencil brushes of good quality and sized in proportion to the space being stenciled. Use a separate brush for each color, or clean the brush and allow it to dry completely before reusing it. Clean the brushes with turpentine, blotting the bristles dry with paper toweling; repeat until there is no paint residue on the toweling. Then wash the brushes in warm, soapy water to remove the oily film, and store them upside down.

Before beginning the actual project, practice stenciling the designs on paper to become familiar with the way the paint handles and to discover the shading effects you can achieve. To give depth to designs such as leaves, shade the edges, leaving the centers lighter. For an aged, fade-away effect, use a heavier touch at the base of the motif and a lighter touch at the top. Stencil on freshly painted walls, or wash the walls to remove grease and dust. Use extra wall paint to touch up any smudges that may occur during stenciling.

TIPS FOR THE PLACEMENT OF STENCILED BORDER DESIGNS

Mark long vertical or horizontal placement lines using a chalk-line tool or pencil; snap a light chalk line in a low-contrast color where the stencil plate should be aligned.

Begin stenciling in the most conspicuous corner of the room and work out in both directions; stop stenciling in the corner that is the least conspicuous.

Continue the stenciled design around the room by bending the stencil plate into the corner, then stenciling onto the adjoining wall.

End obvious repeats at corners, whenever possible, by adjusting the spacing slightly between repeats as you approach the corner; any small differences in spacing will not be noticeable.

Begin at the center of the wall when stenciling a prominent design that needs to be centered; adjust the spacing between repeats near the ends, so a motif ends at the corner.

MATERIALS

GENERAL SUPPLIES

- Precut or custom stencil.
- Oil-based stencil paints.
- Stencil brushes.
- Disposable plastic plates and palette knife, for liquid paints.
- Masking tape or spray adhesive.
- Paper towels.
- Turpentine.

FOR CUSTOM STENCILS

- Transparent Mylar® sheets.
- Tracing paper; colored pencils.
- Mat knife; cutting surface, such as a self-healing cutting board or cardboard.
- Fine-point, permanent-ink marking pen.
- Masking tape.

HOW TO MAKE A CUSTOM STENCIL

1 Place tracing paper over design. Allowing 1" to 3" (2.5 to 7.5 cm) border, trace design, simplifying shapes as necessary; for border designs, repeat design for 13" to 18" (33 to 46 cm) length, making sure that the spacing between repeats is consistent.

2 Color the traced design as desired, using colored pencils. Mark placement lines so stencil will be correctly positioned on wall.

(Continued)

HOW TO MAKE A CUSTOM STENCIL (CONTINUED)

3 Position Mylar® sheet over design; secure with tape. Trace areas that will be stenciled in first color, using marking pen; transfer placement lines.

4 Trace the design areas for each additional color on a separate Mylar sheet. To help align the design, outline areas for previous colors, using dotted lines.

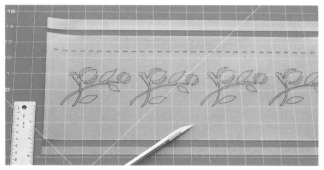

5 Layer Mylar sheets, and check for accuracy. Using mat knife and straightedge, cut outer edges of stencil plates, leaving 1" to 3" (2.5 to 7.5 cm) border around design.

6 Cut out the marked areas, using mat knife; cut the smallest shapes first, then larger ones. Pull knife toward you as you cut; turn Mylar sheet, rather than knife, to change direction.

HOW TO STENCIL USING OIL-BASED STENCIL PAINTS

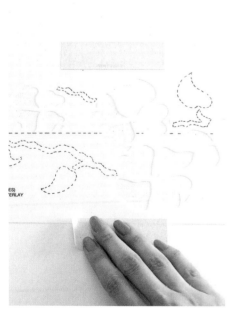

1 Position the first stencil plate; secure the stencil, using masking tape or spray adhesive.

2 **Liquid paint.** Place 1 to 2 tsp. (5 to 10 mL) of paint on plastic plate. Thin the paint, if necessary, until the paint flows back together when a knife is pulled through the paint. Dip tip of stencil brush into paint. Using circular motion, blot brush onto folded paper towel until bristles are almost dry.

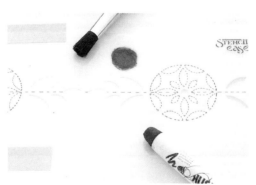

2 **Crayon paint.** Remove protective wax coating from crayon, using paper towel. Rub 1½" (3.8 cm) circle of paint on blank area of stencil plate. Load brush by lightly rubbing brush in circular motion over paint, first in one direction, then in the other.

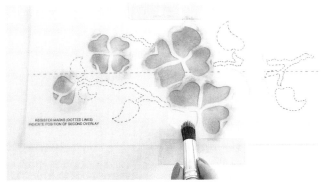

3 Hold stencil plate flat against surface. Holding brush perpendicular to surface and using circular motion, apply a light layer of paint to open areas of stencil.

4 Lift one corner of stencil, and check print; continue applying paint until desired depth of color is achieved in areas of first color. Use all the paint on bristles before adding more paint to brush.

5 Remove first stencil plate. Secure second plate to surface, matching design. Apply second color. Repeat for any remaining stencil plates until design is complete.

6 Touch up any smudges, using background paint and artist's brush. Allow paint to cure for one month. Cured paint may be washed with soap and water.

TECHNIQUES FOR TURNING CORNERS

Mitered corner. Mask off a diagonal line at corner, using masking tape. Stencil one side up to tape; allow the paint to dry. Reposition the tape over edge of stenciled design. Turn stencil plate, and complete motif.

Modified corner. Reposition stencil plate at corners, altering design as needed around corner. This technique can be used for many curved or loosely connected designs.

Interrupted corner. Stencil a single pattern in the corner, using a motif slightly larger in width than border design. Stencil the corners first, then fill in the sides.

MORE IDEAS FOR STENCILING

Stencil, *applied beneath cove molding, creates a border.*

Art Deco motifs *embellish a window frame. The interrupted corner treatment (page 73) adds interest.*

Random motifs, *adapted from upholstery fabric, decorate an area around a window.*

Border of vines and berries *frames the fireplace. The country basket adds a central focal point.*

Greek motifs, *surrounded by wall frame molding (page 66), add a dramatic accent to a transitional room.*

NO-SEW SIDE PANELS

For a simple, no-sew window treatment that has a light, unstructured appearance, drape panels of a soft, lightweight fabric to create a deep valance and elegant floor puddles. This treatment is suitable for full coverage on narrow windows or as side panels on larger windows.

The panels are mounted on swinging extender, or crane, rods, available as antique or contemporary rods. These rods, which extend from about 15" to 22" (38 to 56 cm), can swing out to expose the window view.

Choose a soft, lightweight fabric that appears the same from both sides and has an attractive or minimal selvage. If the fabric ravels, you may want to finish the lower edge of the drapery panel.

CUTTING DIRECTIONS

Measure from the top of the installed rod to the floor. Use one width of fabric for each panel, with the length of each panel equal to the measured distance plus 60" (152.5 cm) to allow for the valance and floor puddle.

HOW TO MAKE DRAPED SIDE PANELS

MATERIALS

- Lightweight fabric, at least 54" (137 cm) wide.
- Swinging extender rod set.
- Double-stick carpet tape.

1 Cut and apply double-stick tape to back side of rod. Drape the upper edge of fabric over rod, with about 4" (10 cm) folded to back side; secure fabric to tape, distributing fullness evenly.

2 Gather the fabric loosely about 36" (91.5 cm) below the rod, using hands; fold bottom of panel up and over rod, with hand gathers at top of rod, forming 18" (46 cm) valance.

3 Arrange the valance, distributing the fullness evenly and folding in the selvages.

4 Arrange bottom of panel on floor, draping it loosely and concealing the raw edges and selvages of the fabric.

GROMMET PANELS
WITH LACING

Grommet panels with lacing are an easy-sew unlined window treatment. Grommets, inserted along the upper edge of the panel, are spaced for a loose, unstructured drape. Hang the panels on a pole set or decorative curtain rod, using cording, ribbon, or leather lacing threaded through the grommets.

Select a soft, lightweight fabric for the best draping results. If the fabric is sheer, reinforce it with nylon net where the grommets are inserted. Insert the grommets yourself with a special attaching tool or have them installed at a tent and awning store or upholstery shop.

The placement of the grommets affects the drape of the panels. For a conventional drape, the end grommets are positioned at the outer corners of the panels; this method must be used if you will be opening and closing the panels or if the rod has a return. To accentuate the unstructured look with draped corners, the end grommets are placed 5" to 8" (12.5 to 20.5 cm) from the corners.

CUTTING DIRECTIONS

Determine the finished panel length by measuring from the bottom of the pole or rod to where you want the lower edge of the curtain; then subtract the space you want between the bottom of the pole and the upper edge of the panel. For floor-length panels, allow ½" (1.3 cm) clearance between the drapery and the floor. For floor puddles, add 18" to 24" (46 to 61 cm).

The cut length of the fabric is equal to the desired finished length of the panel plus 3" (7.5 cm) for the top hem. Also add 8" (20.5 cm) for a double 4" (10 cm) hem at the lower edge; if the panel will be floor-puddled, add only 2" (5 cm) for a double 1" (2.5 cm) hem.

The total cut width of the decorator fabric is equal to two and one-half times the width of the pole or rod. Divide this total in half for two panels, and for each panel, add 6" (15 cm) for side hems. If it is necessary to piece fabric widths together, also add 1" (2.5 cm) for each seam.

Determine the spacing and number of grommets for each curtain panel. The grommets are spaced 10" to 15" (25.5 to 38 cm) apart, depending upon the amount of drape desired between grommets. For draped corners, position the end grommets in from the outer corners a distance equal to one-half the width of the spacing between grommets.

HOW TO MAKE GROMMET PANELS WITH LACING

MATERIALS

- Lightweight decorator fabric.
- Pole set or decorative curtain rod.
- Size 0, or ¼" (6 mm), grommets; attaching tool.
- Lacing.
- Nylon netting, for reinforcing sheer fabric.

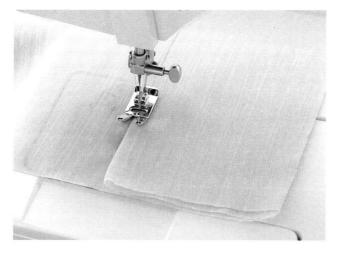

1 Seam fabric widths together for each panel, using ½" (1.3 cm) seam allowance; finish seams. At lower edge of panel, press under 4" (10 cm) twice to wrong side for floor-length panels; press under 1" (2.5 cm) twice for floor-puddled panels. Stitch to make double-fold hem, using straight stitch or blindstitch. (Contrasting thread was used to show detail.)

2 Press under 1½" (3.8 cm) twice on sides. Stitch to make double-fold hems, using straight stitch or blindstitch.

3 Press under 1½" (3.8 cm) twice at upper edge to make double-fold hem. Trim out the excess layers of fabric at corners.

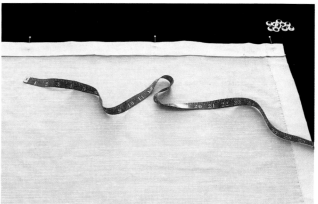

4 Mark the spacing for grommets, placing marks at ends for conventional drape or in from the side edges a distance equal to one-half the width of the spacing for draped corners. Space the remaining grommets evenly between the end markings.

5 Reinforce sheer decorator fabric by positioning a 1½" (3.8 cm) square of net in first fold of upper hem at each grommet marking. Fold and stitch hem, using straight stitch or blindstitch.

6 Fasten grommets securely, using fastening tool; position upper edge of grommets about ½" (1.3 cm) from upper edge of panel. Insert lacing strips through grommets, and tie knots or bows around pole or rod. Install pole.

Ivy window accents *add a romantic touch to a formal swag window treatment (top) or soften the look of a simple pleated shade (inset).*

IVY WINDOW ACCENTS

Embellish formal swags or soften window-shade treatments with silk ivy accents. Honeysuckle vines add interest and provide a base for securing the ivy. The vines are available in coiled bundles at floral shops. Although honeysuckle is rather messy to install, its pliable stems make it easy to work with. Add silk flowers to the arrangement, if desired. Stems with multiple blossoms are easier to arrange than individual flowers.

MATERIALS

- Honeysuckle vines.
- Silk ivy.
- Silk flowers, optional.
- Small screw eyes; medium-gauge wire; wire cutter.

HOW TO MAKE AN IVY WINDOW ACCENT

1 Secure screw eyes in upper edge of window frame, near ends, and spaced at 3 ft. to 4 ft. (0.95 to 1.27 m) intervals. Insert 18" (46 cm) length of wire through each screw eye.

2 Uncoil several of the honeysuckle vines. Starting at one end, wrap the wire around the vines. Twist wire to secure vines, concealing ends of wire.

3 Arrange ivy as desired, tucking the ivy stems into the honeysuckle vines to secure them.

4 Add flowers, if desired, inserting stems with multiple blossoms or individual flowers.

Room
Accents

Make your own table lamps using decorative vases, such as those from ceramic, cut glass, and porcelain. Most vases with a smooth, round top may be converted into a lamp base by drilling a hole in the bottom of the vase. Lamp parts are available at lighting repair stores and hardware stores; follow the simple techniques on pages 86 and 87 for assembly and wiring.

You may drill the hole in the vase yourself or have it drilled for you at a lighting repair or glass supply store. Drilling through ceramic or glass requires a ceramic or diamond drill bit. To help prevent fracturing, place mineral spirits in the well on the bottom of the vase before drilling; this acts as a lubricant and cooling agent. If the bottom of the vase is not recessed, create a well for the mineral spirits, using a glue gun to build up a ridge of hot glue. Keep in mind that there is some risk of fracturing the vase while drilling; for this reason, do not use valuable or irreplaceable pieces.

Select a lamp shade that is in proportion to the vase; often the shade depth is about 2" (5 cm) less than the height of the vase. The lower edge of the lamp shade should be even with the bottom of the harp bracket; select a harp of the correct size for the proper lamp shade placement.

LAMP PARTS

Listed in sequence of assembly:

Plastic cap nut, hex nut, lock washer, and fender washer *secure the end of the lamp pipe under the lamp base.*

Lamp base *is at the bottom of the lamp, with the vase resting on it. So the lamp will sit flat on the table, select a footed lamp base or one with a hole for inserting the electrical cord. Lamp bases are available in a variety of styles, in materials such as brass, wood, and marble.*

Lamp pipe *is inserted through a hole drilled into the bottom of the vase. It supports the lamp parts, and the electrical cord is passed through the hollow pipe.*

Vase cap *covers the top of the vase. Vase caps are available in a variety of finishes and in sizes in ⅛" (3 mm) increments.*

Neck *determines the height of the harp bracket and shade. Brass necks are available in many sizes.*

Harp bracket *separates from the harp proper to allow for the socket assembly.*

Lock washer *is positioned above the harp bracket.*

Socket cap *screws onto the lamp pipe, securing the assembly.*

Socket with insulating sleeve and outer shell *is held in place by the socket cap.*

Harp *positions the shade on the lamp. Metal sleeves lock the harp proper into each end of the harp bracket. Harps are available in several heights to accommodate different shade styles.*

Shade *is supported by the harp. In general, choose a shade that is in proportion to the vase; often the shade depth is about 2" (5 cm) less than the height of the vase. The lower edge of the shade should be even with the bottom of the harp bracket. Adjust the height of the harp as necessary for the proper shade placement.*

Finial *holds the shade in place on the harp and can provide a decorative touch. Finial styles range from simple turned metal to ornate filigree or crystal.*

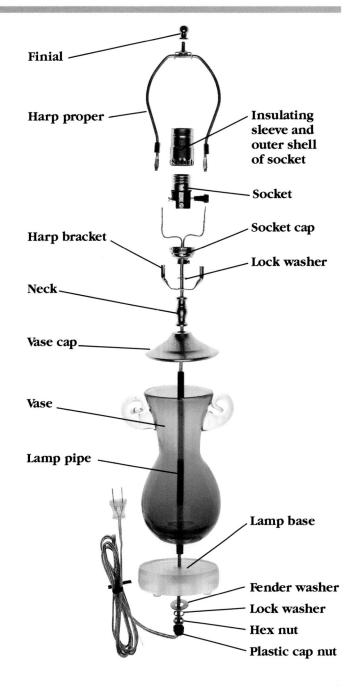

Finial

Harp proper

Insulating sleeve and outer shell of socket

Socket

Harp bracket

Socket cap

Lock washer

Neck

Vase cap

Vase

Lamp pipe

Lamp base

Fender washer

Lock washer

Hex nut

Plastic cap nut

HOW TO MAKE A TABLE LAMP USING A VASE

MATERIALS

- Vase; vase cap to fit top of vase.
- Lamp base; self-adhesive base pad, optional.
- ⅛" IPS lamp pipe; plastic cap nut, hex nut, two lock washers, fender washer.
- Electrical lamp cord with wall plug.
- Socket with 3-way switch, or push-through switch for single-watt bulb.
- Brass neck.

- Harp.
- Lamp shade.
- Finial.
- Drill; ½" (13 mm) ceramic or diamond drill bit; mineral spirits; hot glue gun and glue stick, if necessary.
- Hacksaw, for cutting lamp pipe.
- Screwdriver; utility knife; wire stripper, optional.

1 Place a small amount of mineral spirits in well of vase bottom; make a well, if necessary, with hot glue. Drill a hole in the center of vase bottom, using a ceramic or diamond drill bit; do not apply excessive pressure when drilling.

2 Secure cap nut, hex nut, lock washer, and fender washer to one end of lamp pipe. To determine length of lamp pipe, assemble lamp above fender washer in following order: lamp base, vase, vase cap, neck, harp bracket, and lock washer. Mark a cutting line on pipe ⅜" (1 cm) above lock washer. Disassemble lamp.

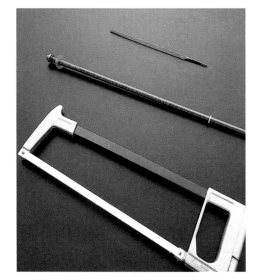

3 Thread hex nut on the pipe, just below cutting line, to act as a cutting guide. Cut pipe at marked line, using a hacksaw. Slowly remove hex nut, straightening any damaged threads. If necessary, file any burrs, using metal file.

4 Reassemble lamp as in step 2. Loosen screw located on the side of the socket cap. Screw socket cap onto lamp pipe; tighten socket cap screw.

5 Insert electrical cord up through lamp pipe, if a footed lamp base is used. For a base with a hole, insert the cord into the hole, then through the lamp pipe.

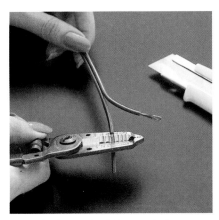

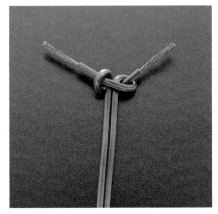

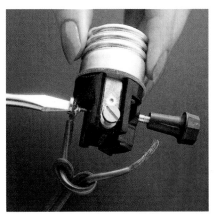

6 Split the end of the cord along the midline of insulation, using utility knife; separate the cord for 2" (5 cm). Remove about ½" to ¾" (1.3 to 2 cm) of insulation from ends, using a wire stripper or knife.

7 Tie an underwriter's knot by forming an overhand loop with one cord and an underhand loop with remaining cord; insert each cord end through the loop of the other cord.

8 Loosen terminal screws on socket. Loop wire on *ribbed side* of cord around silver screw; tighten screw. Loop wire on *rounded side* of cord around gold screw; tighten screw. Make sure all strands of wire are wrapped around screws.

9 Adjust underwriter's knot snug against base of socket; position socket in socket cap. Slide insulating sleeve and outer shell over socket with the terminal screws fully covered and the sleeve slot aligned over the switch.

10 Press socket assembly down into socket cap until socket locks into place. Secure self-adhesive base pad to bottom of lamp base, if necessary.

11 Lift metal sleeves at ends of harp; slide metal sleeves over harp bracket to secure harp. Insert light bulb.

12 Place lamp shade on harp; attach finial.

MORE IDEAS FOR TABLE LAMPS

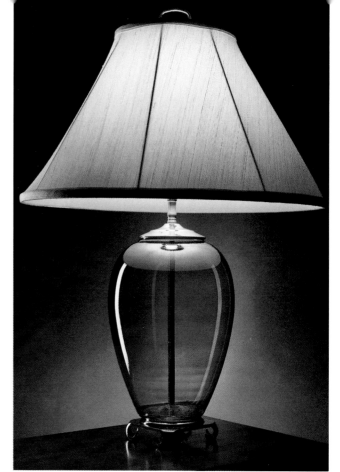

Ginger jar (above), complemented with a linen shade, creates a traditional-style lamp.

Sprinkling can (left) is used instead of a vase for this country-style lamp. The shade is stenciled as on page 70.

Oriental vase (below) rests on an ornate wood base. The opaque shade directs the light downward to highlight the grouping of Chinese items.

Multicolored glass vase (above) is combined with a dark shade for a dramatic effect.

Earthenware vase (right) is supported on a decorative metal base.

Cut-glass vase (below) creates a classic lamp when teamed with a pleated shade. For clear lamps, use a brass lamp pipe with threaded ends.

MATTING & FRAMING

Create your own mats for prints, photographs, or textile artwork and frame the pieces, using simple techniques. The artwork is matted with either a single or double mat, then mounted on a backing board and framed. With a few basic tools, you can achieve professional results.

Art supply stores and framing shops offer framing supplies. Hardware stores supply and cut single-strength glass, an inexpensive and distortion-free glass suitable for most artwork.

Use a mat cutter for cutting mats with a 45° beveled edge. Mat cutters are available in a variety of styles and prices. For best results, select one that has a retractable blade and is marked with a start-and-stop line. Specific cutting instructions may vary with the type of mat cutter.

To preserve photographs or prints, use mat and backing boards that are acid-free; these boards are coated with a buffer to neutralize the acid in the wood pulp. When framing pieces that are valuable or irreplaceable, purchase museum-quality boards made from 100 percent cotton rag.

Select mat boards in textures and colors that complement and enhance the artwork without distracting from it. Many pieces are attractively framed with a single mat, but you may choose a double mat to add depth to a picture. Usually, the color of the outer mat echoes a dominant color in the picture, while the color of the inner mat accentuates interesting features and leads the eye toward the picture.

The width of the outer mat varies with the size of the print and the desired look; experiment, using strips of paper, to determine the desired width. Avoid using frames and mats of the same width; generally, the outer mat is at least twice the width of the frame. In most cases, all four borders of the mat are of equal width. For traditional prints, the lower border is often cut ¼" to ¾" (6 mm to 2 cm) wider than the other three. Contemporary prints often have unequal borders.

When cutting mats and backing boards, measure the inside mounting space of the frame, and cut the backing and outer mat board ⅛" (3 mm) smaller to allow ease for fitting. If you are ordering a custom frame, the fitting ease will be allowed when the frame is cut; specify the exact size of the backing and outer mat boards.

To prevent a print or photograph from warping, choose a firm backing board in a thickness suitable for the frame. For frames with a shallow mounting space, use a heavyweight ply board. For deeper frames, you can use a board with a foam core to provide a lightweight backing.

Select a frame that is in proportion to the picture, making sure that the frame will support the weight of the glass and has the correct mounting space for the thickness of the mats and backing.

Hinge mounting is the preferred method used by professionals for mounting photographs and prints. It is a quick, easy method that uses tape to secure the picture to the backing board. To preserve a valuable photograph or print, use a special framer's tape to secure the picture. Other tapes, such as transparent tape or masking tape, may lose adhesive quality over time and cause the photograph or print to yellow.

Pictures may also be dry-mounted at a framing shop. This permanent type of mounting is especially recommended for lightweight prints, such as posters, that have a tendency to bubble or ripple.

Textile artwork, such as a lace doily, may be mounted by securing it to a mounting board at several points with small hand stitches. Mat board makes a good mounting board and is available in a variety of colors and textures. When framing textiles, make sure that the glass does not touch the cloth; this may require a frame with a deep mounting space.

- Mat board.
- Double-stick framer's tape, for double mat.
- Framer's tape, for hinge mount.

- Mounting board, for mounting textile artwork.
- Backing board.
- Mat cutter; utility knife; cork-backed metal straightedge.

HOW TO CUT A SINGLE MAT

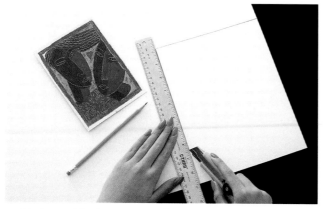

1 Mark outside dimensions of mat on wrong side of mat board, making sure corners are square. Using utility knife and straightedge, score along marked line; repeat until board is cut through.

2 Mark width of mat borders, measuring from each edge and making two marks on each side. Using a sharp pencil and a straightedge, draw lines connecting marks; extend lines almost to edge of board.

3 Place a scrap of mat board under the area to be cut. Using straightedge, align edge of mat cutter with marked line, placing the start-and-stop line (arrow) of cutter even with lower border line.

4 Push the blade into mat. Cut on marked line in one smooth pass; stop when start-and-stop line (arrow) meets upper border line. Pull blade out of mat. Repeat to cut remaining sides.

HOW TO CUT A DOUBLE MAT

1 Cut outer mat as in steps 1 to 4 for single mat, above. Reposition cutout section from outer mat for support when cutting.

2 Cut outside dimensions of mat board for inner mat ¼" (6 mm) smaller than the outer mat.

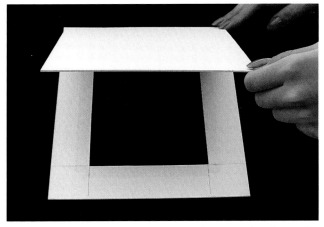

3 Place double-stick framer's tape along inside edges of outer mat, on back side. Place inner mat, face down and centered, over back side of outer mat.

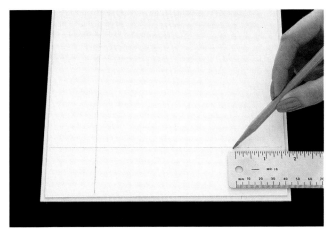

4 Mark width of inner mat borders, measuring from the outside edge of outer mat; this will help ensure even edges. Cut inner mat.

HOW TO HINGE-MOUNT A PICTURE

1 Cut the mat board, opposite. Place the picture on a smooth surface, facing up. Cut two strips of framer's tape about 1" (2.5 cm) long; secure one-half the length of each strip at upper edge on back of picture, as shown, positioning the tape near the ends.

2 Place mat board, face up, over the picture, in desired position. Press firmly along upper border of mat to secure tape.

3 Turn mat and picture over; press firmly to secure tape. Secure strip of framer's tape to mat, directly along edge of picture and perpendicular to first strip of tape. Repeat at opposite end.

4 Cut backing board to same size as mat board. Position picture and mat on backing board.

HOW TO MOUNT TEXTILE ARTWORK

2 Remove textile item; puncture holes at needle markings and again ⅛" (3 mm) from each marking, using awl.

3 Reposition textile item. Using thread that matches textile item, secure it to the mounting board at each set of holes, taking about three stitches. From back of board, tie thread tails, and secure them to board with tape.

1 Cut mat board (page 92); cut the mounting board about 2" (5 cm) larger than mat board. Center the textile item over mounting board. At several locations where article can be supported with small stitches, use a large needle to mark the mounting board by puncturing it.

4 Lift mounting board, and check for proper support of textile item; take additional stitches, if necessary. (Contrasting thread was used to show detail.)

5 Cut strips of double-stick framer's tape; secure to back of mat board along inner edges. Position the mat board over mounting board; press along borders to secure.

6 Cut mounting board even with edges of the mat board, using straightedge and utility knife. Tape strips of mat board to sides of frame, to prevent glass from touching textile item when framed.

HOW TO ASSEMBLE A PICTURE & WOODEN FRAME

MATERIALS

- Wooden picture frame.
- ¾" (2 cm) brads, for attaching frame.
- Framer's fitting tool or slip-joint pliers.
- Brown craft paper; double-stick framer's tape.
- Two screw eyes or one sawtooth hanger.
- Self-adhesive felt or foam bumpers.
- Small awl; braided picture wire; masking tape.

1 Mat and mount picture as on pages 92 and 93. Clean both sides of glass thoroughly, using glass cleaner and lint-free cloth. Position the glass over picture and backing board, with edges even; do not slide glass over surface of the mat. Position frame over glass.

2 Slide fingers under backing board, and turn frame over. Insert ¾" (2 cm) brads into middle of each side of frame, using framer's fitting tool **(a).** Or use slip-joint pliers **(b),** protecting outside edge of frame with strip of cardboard.

a

b

4 Attach double-stick framer's tape to back of frame, about ⅛" (3 mm) from outside edges. Cut brown craft paper 2" (5 cm) larger than frame; place paper on back of frame, securing it to center of each edge of frame and stretching paper taut.

3 Recheck the face of picture for lint or dust; remove brads and clean the glass again, if necessary. Insert brads along each side, 1" (2.5 cm) from corners and at about 2" (5 cm) intervals.

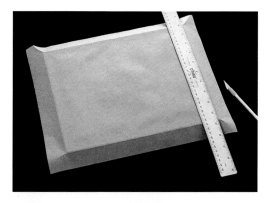

5 Working from the center out to each corner, stretch paper and secure to frame. Crease paper over outside edge of frame. Using a straightedge and utility knife, trim paper about ⅛" (3 mm) inside the creased line.

6 Mark placement for screw eyes, using an awl, about one-third down from upper edge; secure screw eyes into the frame. Thread wire two or three times through one screw eye; twist the end. Repeat at opposite side, allowing slack; wire is usually about 2" to 3" (5 to 7.5 cm) from top of the frame when hung.

7 Cover ends of wire with masking tape. Secure foam bumpers or self-adhesive felt to back of frame, at lower corners.

IDEAS FOR MATTING & FRAMING PICTURES

Grouping of pictures *rests on a wooden display ledge.*

Ribbon, *folded and applied at the corners of the mat board, enhances a romantic print.*

Prints of Chinese calligraphy *(left) are displayed in large, asymmetrical mats for a contemporary look.*

French matting *uses strips of marbleized paper to emphasize the hues of a print. Secure the paper strips with double-stick tape.*

Stenciled design *(page 70) adds a flourish to the mat board of this picture.*

Metallic chart tape *is a simple border for the matted picture at right.*

DECORATOR PILLOWS

Pillows are an excellent way to add accent colors or unusual textures to your living room decorating scheme. Nestled on sofas and armchairs, pillows help create a warm, inviting atmosphere.

In traditional rooms, pillows are an inexpensive way to use lavish fabrics and trims for a touch of elegance and sophistication. In contemporary rooms, colorful pillows can liven up neutral or solid-colored upholstery pieces.

Knife-edge pillows are quick to make; a simple stitched closure allows the pillow to be decorative on both sides. If desired, emphasize the edges of the pillow by attaching a fringe; most fringes have a decorative heading and may be hand-stitched in place. Another way to trim a pillow is by inserting a twisted welting into the seam at the edges of the pillow.

A variety of other trims, such as braid and gimp, may be applied to the front of a decorator pillow. These trims may be topstitched onto the pillow front before the pillow is assembled.

Pillow forms with polyester fiberfill or down filling are available in a variety of sizes. You may also make your own pillow form, sewing the liner as you would a knife-edge pillow and filling it with polyester fiberfill.

MATERIALS

- Decorator fabric.
- Pillow form.
- Polyester fiberfill, for filling out corners.
- Decorative trim, such as twisted welting or fringe, optional.

HOW TO MAKE A BASIC KNIFE-EDGE PILLOW

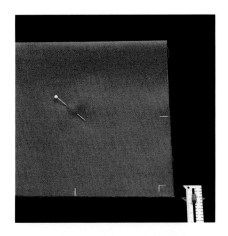

1 Cut pillow front and pillow back 1" (2.5 cm) wider and longer than the pillow form. Fold the pillow front into fourths. Mark a point halfway between corner and fold on each open side. At the corner, mark a point ½" (1.3 cm) from each raw edge.

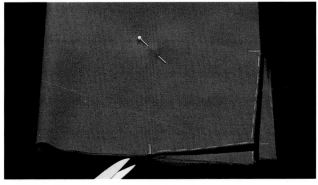

2 Mark lines, tapering from raw edges at center marks to marks at corner. Cut on marked lines.

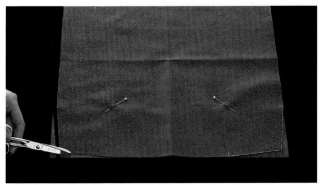

3 Use pillow front as pattern for cutting pillow back so all corners are tapered. This will eliminate dog-eared corners on the finished pillow.

4 Pin pillow front to pillow back, right sides together. Stitch ½" (1.3 cm) seam, leaving opening on one side for turning and for inserting pillow form.

(Continued)

5 Turn pillow cover right side out, pulling out the corners. Press under seam allowances at opening.

6 Insert pillow form; push fiberfill into the corners of the pillow as necessary to fill out pillow.

7 Pin opening closed; slipstitch or edgestitch close to folded edge.

HOW TO ATTACH TRIMS

Trim without decorative heading. Machine-baste trim to right side of pillow front, with heading of fringe within seam allowance. At ends, cut fringe between loops and hand-stitch loop to secure it; butt ends together. Place pillow front and pillow back right sides together; machine-stitch. Insert pillow form.

Trim with decorative heading. Pin trim around outer edge of pillow cover; miter heading at corners by folding trim at an angle. Hand-stitch along both edges of the trim and along the diagonal fold of mitered corners. Insert pillow form.

HOW TO ATTACH TWISTED WELTING

1 Identify right side of twisted welting; from right side, inner edge of tape is not visible. Stitch twisted welting to *pillow back,* using zipper foot, with right sides up and outer edge of welting tape aligned to raw edge of fabric. Leave 1½" (3.8 cm) unstitched between the ends; leave 3" (7.5 cm) tails.

2 Remove stitching from welting tape on tails. Separate the cords; wrap transparent tape around ends to prevent raveling. Trim ends of the welting tape to 1" (2.5 cm) from stitching; overlap the ends, and secure with transparent tape. Arrange cords so those at right turn up and those at left turn down.

3 Insert cords at right end under the welting tape, twisting them and pulling them down until the welting is returned to its original shape. Secure in place, using tape or pins.

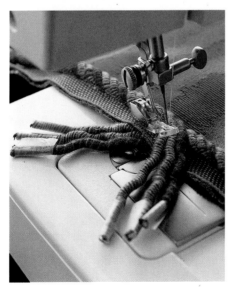

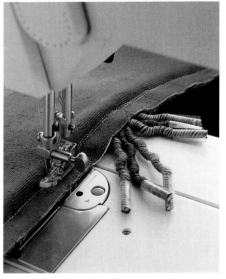

4 Twist and pull cords at left end over cords at right end until the twisted ends look like continuous twisted welting; check both sides of the welting.

5 Position zipper foot on left side of needle; this will allow you to stitch in the direction of the twists. Machine-baste through all layers to secure the welting at the seamline. Cords may be hand-basted in place, if desired.

6 Place pillow back on pillow front, right sides together. Stitch as close to welting as possible, using zipper foot; leave opening for turning. With pillow front facing up, stitch again, crowding stitches closer to welting.

MORE IDEAS FOR DECORATOR PILLOWS

Banded inset *is the focal point of the velveteen pillow shown above. For added detail, twisted welting edges the pillow, and tassels adorn the corners.*

Decorative cording, *cinched and tied around the simple knife-edge pillows at left, adds detailing. The ends of the cording are finished with end caps.*

Decorative panels *enhance the pillows below. One pillow features a center fabric panel accented with antique lace and buttons; another has a purchased tapestry panel. Gimp, topstitched over the edges, frames the panels.*

Long, twisted fringe drapes gracefully along the sides of the rectangular pillow above.

Strips of leather lacing, woven together, are inserted into the seams at one corner of the pillow at left. Beads, woven in randomly, add color.

Luxurious tassels add an elegant touch to the corners of simple pillows.

PAINTED FLOOR CLOTHS

Express your creativity by making a custom floor cloth with decorative painting or stenciling. Used at the entryway to the living room or as an area rug, a floor cloth can become an artwork conversation piece.

When designing the floor cloth, you may want to browse through art books or quilt books for design ideas and use a photocopy machine to enlarge the design to the desired size. Or duplicate a design used elsewhere in the room, such as a fabric or wallpaper design. For a perfect color match, have the paint colors for the floor cloth custom-mixed to match the fabric or wallpaper swatches.

An 18-ounce (500 gram) or #8 canvas provides a durable surface for floor cloths and lies flat on the floor. It is available in widths up to 5 feet (152.5 centimeters) at tent and awning stores and upholstery shops.

Paint the canvas, using latex paints intended for floors and patios. These paints are very durable and can be custom-mixed by the quart (0.9 liter). Or stencil the canvas, using oil-based paint crayons designed for stenciling; this type of paint will not bleed when applied to the fabric. To protect the floor cloth from abrasion, seal it with a nonyellowing latex urethane acrylic finish.

If the rug will be placed on a smooth floor surface, such as linoleum or ceramic, place a nonslip pad under the floor cloth.

HOW TO MAKE A PAINTED FLOOR CLOTH

MATERIALS

- 18-oz. (500 g) or #8 canvas.

- Latex floor paints in desired colors, paint roller, roller tray, and paintbrushes, for painted floor cloth.

- Oil-based paint crayons and stencil brushes, for stenciled floor cloth.

- Sealer, such as a nonyellowing latex urethane acrylic finish.

- Synthetic-bristle paintbrush, for applying sealer.

- Plastic drop cloth; carpenter's square; straightedge.

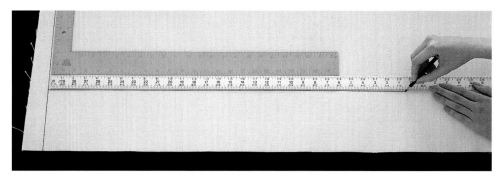

1 Trim selvages from canvas. Mark canvas to desired size, using pencil, carpenter's square, and straightedge; cut canvas.

2 Machine-stitch around the canvas ¼" (6 mm) from raw edges; stitch a second row of stitching ⅛" (3 mm) from raw edges. Press canvas so it lies flat.

3 Place canvas on a plastic drop cloth. Using paint roller, apply background color of paint, taking care not to crease canvas; roll paint in all directions to penetrate fabric. Allow to dry. Apply additional coats as necessary; allow to dry overnight. Trim any loose threads.

4 Mark design, if desired, using pencil. Paint desired design, applying one color at a time. Use a fine-pointed brush for outlining and wider brush for filling in design areas. Allow paint to dry 24 hours.

5 Apply sealer, using synthetic-bristle paintbrush; allow to dry several hours. Apply two additional coats of sealer, following manufacturer's instructions for drying time.

Stenciled floor cloth. Prepare the canvas as in steps 1 and 2, opposite. Stencil design as on pages 70 to 73. Apply sealer as in step 5, left.

MORE IDEAS FOR PAINTED FLOOR CLOTHS

Quilt design has been enlarged for this floor cloth.

Geometric fabric design was mimicked to create a coordinating floor cloth.

Stenciled rug *echoes the design applied to the walls.*

HANDMADE
PAPER ACCENTS

Create one-of-a-kind accessories, such as wall collages, bowls, and vases, from handmade paper. The craft of papermaking requires minimal equipment and supplies.

To make handmade paper, a pulp is prepared in a blender, then poured into a vat. A layer of paper fibers is lifted from the solution in the vat, using a mesh screen and frame called a *mold and deckle*. After draining off the water, *couch* (pronounced "cooch") the paper by inverting it onto a smooth cloth and compressing the fibers.

Many products may be used for making the pulp for handmade paper. For a strong, high-quality paper, use cotton linters; these ready-made sheets of cotton fibers are available at fiber-art stores and through mail-order suppliers. Paper, such as old letters and cards, newspaper, computer paper, construction paper, and grocery bags, may also be used. Avoid recycled paper or paper with a shiny surface. The color of the handmade paper will be determined by the pieces used for the pulp. Experiment with mixing different types of papers for the pulp to create handmade papers in a variety of textures and colors. Fabric dyes that are suitable for use in warm water may also be added to the pulp mixture.

HOW TO MAKE THE MOLD & DECKLE

MATERIALS

- Stretcher bars in four 9" (23 cm) lengths and four 12" (30.5 cm) lengths; or use desired sizes.
- Fiberglass window screening.
- ½" (1.3 cm) hardware cloth.
- Duct tape.
- Polyurethane varnish, optional.
- Staple gun; rustproof staples; wire cutter; wood glue.

1 Assemble two 9" × 12" (23 × 30.5 cm) frames from stretcher bars, making sure corners fit tightly and are squared; secure each joint with wood glue and a staple. If desired, apply one or two coats of polyurethane varnish; allow to dry. Set aside one frame. This frame is the deckle.

2 Cut the hardware cloth to fit the remaining frame, using a wire cutter; secure to frame at center of each side with a staple.

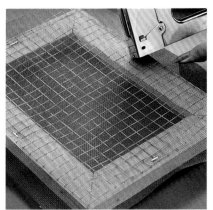

3 Cut window screening 1" (2.5 cm) larger than frame on all four sides; place over hardware cloth, and staple to the frame at center of each side, pulling screening taut.

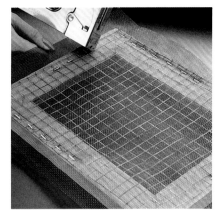

4 Continue to staple screening to frame, working from center of each side to corners and pulling it taut; place staples at 1" (2.5 cm) intervals.

5 Trim excess screening. Apply the duct tape over staples, wrapping the tape around sides of frame. This frame is the mold.

MATERIALS

- Cotton linters or paper product (page 109), for making pulp.
- Cotton sheeting or nonwoven interfacing, for couching surface.
- Bucket.
- Vat, at least 6" (15 cm) deep.
- Blender.
- Sponge; strainer or colander.

1 Tear cotton linter or paper product into small pieces, about 1" (2.5 cm) square. Place pieces in bucket filled with hot water; allow to soak overnight.

2 Fill vat about half full with warm water. Spread cotton sheeting or nonwoven interfacing on smooth, flat surface for couching. Strain cotton linter pieces, using strainer or colander.

3 Pour about 2 c. (0.47 L) water into blender. Add about 10 to 15 pieces of cotton linter. Blend, using short bursts of speed, until cotton linter becomes pulp; do not overwork blender. Pour pulp into vat.

4 Continue making pulp and adding it to the vat until mixture in vat is a slurry consistency. Stir the mixture well, using hands.

5 Place deckle over screen side of mold. Hold edges firmly on the two short sides, and immerse mold vertically into one end of the vat; tilt mold horizontally, moving it along the bottom of the vat to opposite end. Keeping mold level, lift it out of vat.

6 Shake mold gently from side to side, evenly dispersing fibers; keep mold level. Allow excess water to drain into the vat, holding the mold slightly tilted.

7 Remove deckle, taking care that water does not drip from deckle onto the sheet of pulp.

8 Place mold, pulp side down, on cotton sheeting. Couch to remove excess moisture and compress fibers, using sponge. Remove mold.

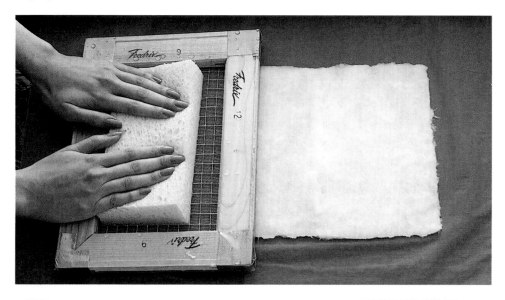

9 Repeat steps 5 to 8 for additional sheets, stirring mixture well each time before dipping frame into vat. Larger sheets may be made by overlapping the edges and compressing seams, using sponge. Add more pulp to the vat after every three or four sheets are made.

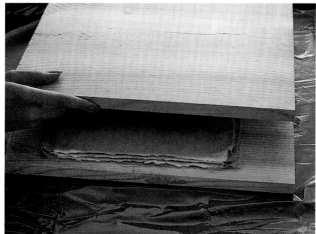

10 Allow paper to dry. For smooth, flat finish, allow it to air dry several hours; then place damp sheets of paper between layers of cotton sheeting. Place paper and cotton sheeting between weighted boards.

11 Strain excess pulp from vat, using strainer or colander; do not pour pulp down any drain. Squeeze pulp to remove excess water; discard. Or to reuse pulp, allow it to air dry; dried pulp must be resoaked before it is used again.

TECHNIQUES FOR ADDING TEXTURE TO HANDMADE PAPER

Embellishing. Add items such as decorative threads, dried or fresh petals, leaves, and grasses to the vat. Or, apply items to paper after couching, securing them with pulp.

Draping. Manipulate paper while it is damp by lifting and draping it to create folds and creases. Support folds as necessary, using crumpled sheets of plastic wrap or wax paper.

Embossing. Press items such as wire grids, tracing wheels, and kitchen utensils on freshly couched paper.

HOW TO MAKE A PAPER COLLAGE

1 Make several sheets of paper (pages 110 to 111) in various sizes and shapes; paper may be torn into smaller pieces or shaped while damp.

2 Paint paper, if desired, using a light coat of aerosol paint.

4 Mount collage by stitching each piece to mounting board (page 94); start with background piece, working toward top layer. Conceal stitches by stitching in areas where stitches will be overlapped by the next layer.

3 Experiment with layering sheets of paper in different positions until a pleasing arrangement is achieved.

5 Stitch or glue any embellishments, such as hardware cloth, beads, and buttons, to paper. Frame collage (pages 90 to 95), using a shadow-box frame.

HOW TO MAKE A BOWL OR VASE FROM HANDMADE PAPER

1 Apply a thin layer of liquid soap to the inside of bowl or vase. Gather pulp in mold; drain off excess water.

2 Press handfuls of pulp against sides and bottom of bowl; compress pulp, using fingers and knuckles. Use a sponge to remove excess water periodically and to smooth the inner surface. Allow paper to dry; paper will pull away from bowl.

IDEAS FOR HANDMADE PAPER

Woven strips of handmade paper (left), secured to a large background sheet, are used for this framed artwork. Decorative threads are tied to the woven strips of paper.

Wall hanging (below) is created with hardware cloth used as the foundation. Couch the handmade paper onto a piece of hardware cloth. After allowing the paper to partially dry, shape the hardware cloth as desired by bending it. The watercolor effect is achieved by painting the paper with an airbrush.

Framed paper collage (above) in neutral tones is accented with bits of metal.

Bowls and vases (below) in a variety of shapes and sizes are displayed as a grouping. The bowl at right consists of two bowls, with bases glued together; twisted cording adds the finishing touch.

FLORAL BUNDLES

Long-stemmed dried naturals bundled in decorative containers make simple, attractive arrangements. Several bundles of various heights can be grouped for added impact.

For tall floral bundles, select a container that is heavy enough to support the height of the plant. If necessary, weight the bottom of the container with rocks or sand.

HOW TO MAKE A FLORAL BUNDLE

MATERIALS

- Dried naturals, such as roses, lavender, or rye.
- Decorative container.
- Floral arranging foam, such as by The John Henry Company.
- Sheet moss or Spanish moss; floral pins.
- 1½ yd. (1.4 m) ribbon or paper twist, optional.

1 Cut floral foam, using knife, so foam fits container snugly and is about ½" (1.3 cm) from top; cut and insert foam wedges as necessary. Cover foam with moss, securing it with floral pins.

2 Insert stems of dried naturals into foam, starting in center and working out in a circle until desired fullness is achieved. Stems in the outer rows may be shorter than in the center.

3 Wrap a ribbon or paper twist around the bundle, if desired; tie in a bow.

Tiered bundle of dried naturals (above) is arranged in an oval container. The bay leaves and pomegranates at the base of the stems add a finishing touch.

Wheat bundle (left) is arranged in the usual manner, then tied tightly and twisted to give it a new shape. Dried hydrangeas are clustered above the basket.

MORE IDEAS FOR FLORAL BUNDLES

Bundle of grain and flowers is arranged in a small, aged terra cotta pot. The bow is tied close to the pot, allowing the grain to flare gently.

Tiers of roses and cockscomb are simply arranged in a decorative pot.

Tiny dried roses are arranged in a small metal pot.

WILLOW
ARRANGEMENTS

Arrangements of dried branches are a popular room accent. Curly willow branches are especially attractive because of their gnarled, twisted look. Available from floral shops, the freshly harvested branches of curly willow are green, but will dry to shades of brown.

Willow branches can be displayed in various containers, from large ceramic pots to shallow willow baskets. Choose a container that complements the decorating scheme of the room. To secure the branches firmly, the willow arrangement is set in plaster of Paris.

HOW TO MAKE A WILLOW ARRANGEMENT

MATERIALS

- Curly willow branches.
- Sheet moss or Spanish moss.
- Decorative container.

- Plaster of Paris; disposable container for mixing.
- Cardboard; string or rubber bands.
- Heavy-duty aluminum foil.

1 Line container loosely with two layers of aluminum foil. If foil shows through sides of container, place moss between foil and container.

2 Cut cardboard to fit bottom of container; insert over foil. Cardboard will prevent branches from puncturing the foil. Trim branches to the desired height, cutting them at the base. Secure lower portion of branches together, using string or rubber bands.

3 Mix the plaster of Paris, following the manufacturer's instructions. Pour plaster into pot; plaster should be at least 4" (10 cm) deep. When the plaster starts to thicken, insert branches. Support branches until plaster has set.

4 Fold excess foil over plaster. Conceal plaster with moss. If using deep container, fill with crumpled newspaper; then add moss. Remove string or rubber bands after 24 hours.

TABLESCAPES

Groupings of interesting accessories, placed in artful arrangements on coffee tables and side tables, add a finishing touch to living rooms. Often called "tablescapes," these arrangements provide an opportunity to showcase small or sentimental objects that otherwise might go unnoticed. Use your creativity to create tablescapes with a personal touch.

Objects in tablescapes need not be expensive. Look around your home for unique items such as pottery or porcelain pieces, decorative boxes, and seashells. Small plants, a stack of books, and family photographs can also be attractive additions to table arrangements.

Try grouping objects of various shapes, sizes, and textures, moving the objects around to find the most eye-pleasing arrangement. Repeat some feature, such as color, shape, or texture, in several pieces, to give a feeling of unity, and vary the height of the objects for visual interest.

Rich brown tones *unify the items in this traditional tablescape. The varied sizes and shapes of the pieces add interest.*

Pairs of accessories are used to create this transitional tablescape. Although most items are in related colors, bold yellow adds contrast.

Bold colors are unified by a multicolored vase. This contemporary tablescape uses accessories in a mix of interesting shapes. The eggplant adds an element of surprise.

Old-fashioned country look is achieved by combining sentimental treasures with modern reproductions.

COLLECTIONS

Displays of collections add a personal touch to rooms, reflecting the personalities of the people who live there. Whether your collections are simple seashells or fine porcelain figurines, items that hold meaning for you are worthy of attention.

To call attention to collections, display the items in a grouping; scattered around the room, they lose their impact. Shelves, bookcases, and mantels are ideal for displaying many types of collections. Glass-enclosed display cases protect fragile objects. When arranging items, keep scale and balance in mind, taking care not to overcrowd them. If items are too small to hold their own, add other pieces for balance. Use spot or accent lighting to highlight the display.

Decanters (left) are artistically grouped on a side table.

Candlesticks (right) create an interesting linear arrangement on any tabletop or mantel.

Collectible picture frames contain mirrors, rather than artwork, to create a unified wall display.

Primitive wooden figures, *African in origin, command attention on the mantel in a transitional room.*

Handwoven baskets
*from a traveler's collection
are displayed on the hearth
of a fireplace at right. These
one-of-a-kind baskets add
textural interest to the room.*

Contemporary pieces
*of earthenware and
glassware (below), each
unique in handcrafted
beauty, are prominently
displayed as a tablescape
(page 122).*

INDEX

CREDITS

CY DECOSSE INCORPORATED
Chairman: Cy DeCosse
President: James B. Maus
Executive Vice President:
 William B. Jones

DECORATING THE LIVING ROOM
Created by: The Editors of
 Cy DeCosse Incorporated

Also available from the publisher:
 *Bedroom Decorating, Creative Window
 Treatments, Decorating for Christmas,
 Decorating with Silk & Dried Flowers,
 Decorating the Kitchen, Kitchen &
 Bathroom Ideas, Decorative Painting,
 Decorating your Home for Christmas,
 Decorating for Dining & Entertaining*

Executive Editor: Zoe A. Graul
Technical Director: Rita C. Opseth
Project Manager: Joseph Cella
Assistant Project Manager: Diane
 Dreon-Krattiger
Senior Art Director: Lisa Rosenthal
Art Director: Brad Springer
Writer: Rita C. Opseth
Editor: Janice Cauley
Sample Supervisor: Carol Olson

Photo Coordinator: Diane Dreon-Krattiger
Technical Photo Director: Bridget
 Haugh
Styling Director: Bobbette Destiche
Crafts Stylist: Joanne Wawra
Research Assistant: Lori Ritter
Artisans: Ray Arndt, Sr., Phyllis
 Galbraith, Bridget Haugh, Sara
 Macdonald, Linda Neubauer, Carol
 Pilot, Nancy Sundeen
*Director of Development Planning
 & Production:* Jim Bindas
Photo Studio Managers: Mike Parker,
 Cathleen Shannon
Assistant Studio Manager: Rena Tassone
Lead Photographer: Mike Parker
Photographers: Rex Irmen, John
 Lauenstein, Bill Lindner, Paul Najlis
Contributing Photographers: Phil
 Aarestad, Kim Bailey, Rebecca
 Hawthorne, Paul Herda, Charles
 Nields, Brad Parker, Marc Scholtes
Photo Stylist: Susan Pasqual
Production Manager: Amelia Merz
Electronic Publishing Specialist: Joe Fahey
Production Staff: Adam Esco, Jeff
 Hickman, Mike Schauer, Nik Wogstad
Shop Supervisor: Phil Juntti

Scenic Carpenters: Curtis Lund, John
 Nadeau, Tom Rosch, Greg Wallace
Consultants: Ray Arndt, Sr., Amy Engman,
 Pam Enz, Dee Ginther, Carolyn
 Golberg, Wendy Fedie, Letitia Little,
 Lindsey Peterson, Peter van Dyke,
 Verna von Goltz, Donna Whitman
Contributors: Coats & Clark Inc.; Conso
 Products Company; Dritz Corporation;
 Dyno Merchandise Corporation; Lisa
 Ellias, The Gathering; P. G. Gravele, MJL
 Impressions; Putman Company; The
 Singer Company; Stencil Ease;
 Swiss-Metrosene, Inc.; Watson Smith;
 Waverly, Division of F. Schumacher
 & Company
Printed on American paper by: R.R.
 Donnelley & Sons Co. (0395)

Cy DeCosse Incorporated offers a variety of
how-to books. For information write:
 Cy DeCosse Subscriber Books
 5900 Green Oak Drive
 Minnetonka, MN 55343